CL

MW00961997

7

Bring on your Greatness!

~ The World Messenger

The World Messenger
From Fear to Greatness:
Business, Sports, & Life Lessons

IZABELA LUNDBERG

INTERNATIONAL #1 BESTSELLER

Game on, Champ!

Izabela

P.S. Keep up with great work!

The World Messenger. 1st Edition. 2015

ISBN-13: 978-1511871006
ISBN-10: 1511871008
Amazon Kindle: B00X94YOD8
Ingram Spark: 978-1943845149

DEDICATION

*This book is inspired by all the people who have given me
So much unconditional love and support,
This is especially for those who believed in me early on in my life...*

*When I was young and searching for my identity
During times of loneliness and my struggle to find beauty,
When beauty was often lost in a maze of conflict, horror, and war.*

*As I traveled the world and met every one of you on my journey
Love would find me and envelop me,
But only when the door of my heart was open to it.*

*Years ago, **I** tore down that door
And in its place, I built an archway
That is always open to **LOVE**.*

*May this book find its way to the doorway of your heart
And inspire you to achieve the greatness that lives inside of **YOU**!*

*I dedicate this book in loving memory of my exceptional parents, my
mentor – grandma Angela, to the people of the former Yugoslavia, and
to those around the world who lost their lives in their efforts for love
and freedom.*

BOOK TESTIMONIES

"The path to set you to your destiny is in your hands! Izabela shows you how to go from where you are where you are destined to go. Read it, apply it and arrive at your destiny!"

~ Douglas Weiss P.h. D.
Psychiatrist, Author & Speaker

"Izabela Lundberg shares a message of hope and healing that people all over our planet need to hear. And heed. Listen closely."

~ Greg S. Reid
Best Selling Author of Think and Grow Rich "Stickability": The Power of Perseverance, Three Feet From Gold, Close to the Finish Line, The Rise, etc.

"When you read Izabela Lundberg's, The World Messenger, you will come away inspired to take positive action immediately. Izabela's ability to integrate stories and messages provide you with the concepts of how to create the mindset which will move you forward in business, sports and life."

~ Coach Sherry Winn
Two-time Olympian
National Championship Basketball Coach
The Originator of the WIN Philosophy

"If you're ready to positively transform your life, then read and absorb the strategies in this brilliant book by Izabela Lundberg. Izabela truly cares about helping others and her ideas will make a positive difference in your life!"

~ James Malinchak
Featured on ABCs Hit TV Show, "Secret Millionaire"
Author of the Top-Selling Book, Millionaire Success Secrets
Founder, www.BigMoneySpeaker.com

"I was moved by your book especially the stories of people you met related to your life and work, Izabela. What an inspiring and timely role model you are for what is again happening in the world."

~ Kare Anderson
Author, Keynote Speaker and Forbs & Huffington Post Columnist

"Izabela Lundberg's engaging story is one of big dreams, amazing persistence, powerful drive, and creative adaptability. Izabela brings a unique perspective to "battling one's way to the top." She survived a brutal civil war in her homeland with her passionate commitment to making her dreams come true, no matter the odds.

She is a true world messenger. Izabela is a global citizen with a message of hope for every person, no matter their circumstance. You will find guidance, peace, and inspiration in her book."

~ S. Chris Edmonds
Best-selling author of *The Culture Engine and Leading at a Higher Level*

"As Publisher and Executive Editor for BIZCATALYST 360.com (a global business resource portal), I've had the opportunity to preside over the curation, editings, reviewing and publishing of over 11,000 essays in recent years, the vast majority of which focused on Leadership - from virtually every conceivable aspect. Upon reading Izabela's new Book, it was a refreshing surprise and indeed a pleasure to discover a "treasure trove" of unparaled leadership perspectives. What separates Izabela's thought leadership from the rest is her approach - effective drawing "real-world," experienced insights, which provides the reader with actionable intelligence. Bottom line - Izabela has now set the standard for what many refer to but few deliver, that is; authentic LEGACY leadership principles... "

~ Dennis J. Pitocco
Publisher & Executive Editor
BIZCATALYST360.com

THE WORLD MESSENGER BOOK
FOREWORD

Listen closely. In this book, Izabela Lundberg shares a message not only of hope and healing, but of help for a hurting world.

A message not only of struggle at the lowest levels, but of success at the highest pinnacle.

A message that people all over our planet need to hear. And heed.

I love this book, and I'm grateful that Izabela has so openly, humbly and honestly shared the insights, paths, and practical principles that anyone can adopt to overcome their obstacles and achieve peace of mind and prosperity.

She and I have been privileged to meet many of the most successful, most accomplished, most admired men and women in the world. One thing they all have in common is that they've battled—and ultimately overcome—challenges, difficulties and even threats.

Yet they persevered. And prospered.

Izabela Lundberg uncovers the mindsets and actions that have made them victorious in business, sports and life. And she elucidates those thought patterns and action habits so you, too, can mine your own gold.

But Izabela hasn't only studied other successful people. She, herself walked a harrowing and dangerous path to accomplishment. In her book, you'll see how she embodies the single success trait that is so important, I devoted an entire book to it: Stickability.

In fact, the winning formula is "Stickability-plus-flexibility." Add to that "creativity" plus deep compassion for and commitment to helping others—from trauma and genocide survivors to international C-suite executives and brilliant Olympic level athletes—and you have the global force that is The World Messenger.

This book will inspire you to realize your own inner Olympian.
Listen closely.
And live your Message.

Greg S. Reid
Author of Think and Grow Rich "Stickability": The Power of Perseverance, Three Feet From Gold, Close to the Finish Line, The Way Out, The Rise & others

Contents

In the moments when it seems like
You have nothing left but defeat,
No one by your side to cheer you up,
Pick you up, or give a hand;
Know that YOU CAN keep going!
True warriors on their life's mission
Continue on to greatness!

~ Izabela, The World Messenger

Acknowlegements

They say it takes a village to raise a child. Similarly, I could not have finished this book without help. The content of this book has been living in my head for a while, and now was the perfect time to share it with the world.

I am deeply grateful and very touched by a number of people who have supported me on the journey while writing this book. This process was rewarding, liberating, and empowering despite moments of sadness.

Without advice and editing from particular people, this book would not exist. They challenged my material and enabled me to weave a coherent story.

I would like to thank all the members of my team:

Rebecca Popara, my executive assistant and editor for her incredible service and willingness to go the extra mile.

Yael Cohen for tremendous dedication, strategic feedback, editing services, and support. Her professional consulting experience combined with her love of writing and editing, passion for travel and sports, and dedication to helping others achieve their goals, helped focus me and my writing.

Erik Kulp my dear friend, for exceptional support, insightful editing, and knowledge and passion for sports.

Robert Davis for protecting my Voice while fine-tuning my "music." All thought leaders should seek your magical branding and positioning creativity to help them impact the world with their messages.

Scott Palat for the great advice, outstanding motivation, and inspiring greatness in me. This journey would not be as successful without his unwavering support.

Zoran Kazovic, John North, Pierre-Emmanuel Czaja and Ken Perreault for leadership, friendship, and tremendous support.

And finally, my siblings, Igor, Inga and Iva for your unconditional love!

I greatly appreciate all the professional athletes, coaches, and leadership executives who I interviewed for this book. I gained such a diverse and global perspective by speaking to people from six continents. Unfortunately, not all of you who I interviewed could be included in this book, but by sharing your words of wisdom, inspiration, and motivation with me, it has opened the door for future collaboration, and the creation of books to come.

None of us are perfect, so I would like to acknowledge that any errors you may read are not intentional. However, my message is intentional.

Thank you to my many wonderful family, friends, and mentors who taught me and supported me so much through my best and worst life experiences. My journey would have been impossible to accomplish without you!

Introduction

For many of us, photos or a few moments of a video are the only glimpses of the horrors and atrocities of war, the pain of victims, the guilt of survivors, and the violent aftermath of desolation that we will ever witness. Some of us may even feel moved – but seldom moved to action beyond "liking" or "sharing" the content on social media, or perhaps writing a comment.

But when you've seen and lived through war, the images you see on your smartphone remind you of when you felt the steel of a gun barrel against your forehead, smelled the threatening breath of a drunk soldier, and hid yourself to escape violence. Little did I imagine that as a wide-eyed five year old girl fascinated by the Olympic Games, I would later experience pain and terror that defied the Olympic spirit that I was so enamored with.

In 1991, civil war broke out in my childhood home of Yugoslavia, and my life was turned upside down. It was a conflict that had economic, ethnic, political, and cultural roots. And years later, such conflicts continue to exist around the globe – compelling me to share my story, as a way to connect and not to clash; to build a bridge where we can reconcile and find peace, with the hope of ultimately putting an end to these conflicts and relegating them to the pages of history.

I believe that it is possible to build a bridge with everyone, a bridge of shared understanding and reconciliation, because it is within our power to build that bridge. I envision a future in which we all will be sitting around a table, sharing our stories of love, support, and unity.

Parts of my story are extremely painful for me to relive, but it is my goal to inspire you and millions of other people across the globe to overcome your worst fears and live out your greatness. If I have been able to overcome the things I am about to share with you, you can too. There are solutions to every problem we face, and by focusing your attention on the solutions and not letting fear hold you back, the sky is the limit.

I believe this book, in addition to my short documentary video (IzabelaLundberg.com/author) of how I got to the US, can act and serve as a motivator for you to grow beyond your wildest imagination. You and only you hold the keys to overcoming all of the fears within yourself, your surroundings, and the people around you.

The World Messenger was born within me when I was a child and this book is my effort to share messages of personal and professional development - from my experience as well as from those of some business executives and professional athletes. The World Messenger is on a life journey with defined vision, clarity, and persistence to create over one million legacy leaders in decades to come.

I encourage you to live your life to your fullest potential. Indeed, you can get back up even when no one is there to cheer you on or support you. You can continue to demonstrate leadership and to inspire harmony, service and love among us all, regardless of gender, age, color, nationality, or religion. Life is a continuous journey - make every moment count.

Leave a Legacy - A Legacy That Matters!

~ Izabela Lundberg

Chapter One

Discovering Your Dream

As I lay down in the tall grass on my grandpa's ranch high up in the mountains outside of Sarajevo, engulfed by the breathtaking view of the blue sky and fresh mountain air and fluffy airplane traces, I escaped into daydreams. "Where are these airplanes going?" I wondered. "Who is flying right now? Who are the people? What do they look like? What languages do they speak?"

Was this an unusual daily summer ritual for a soon-to-be five year old? I could not help it. Deep in me I knew that a bigger, greater world existed beyond the little bubble that I was exposed to, making me yearn for more information at all times. I drove my parents and family crazy with millions of questions.

My big dark eyes full of wonder and curiosity would just get bigger as more and more knowledge was poured into my head, leading me day after day with an undying hunger to explore more. To explore the world!

When I was asked in the middle of the summer what I would like for my fifth birthday, I was so excited to tell everyone, "I want a money kit and a football!" My parents, especially my dad, were not surprised at all with my selection. After all I was a cute little tomboy, and they were ready to honor my wish.

A football was an extra gift that I wanted to share with the kids on my street, since balls were often lost in the river, taken by older kids, or slashed by a grumpy old man after we broke his windows for the third or fourth time.

I was ecstatic to get the money kit that consisted of a big cardboard world map, little flags of the countries, and fake currency in the form of paper and coins. I had my favorite treasure, the whole world in front of me with names of countries, currencies, and flags to play with. This was my version of a chess game that I could play with for hours alone. At that moment, deep down without knowing it at the time the World Messenger was born!

I vividly remember lying on the floor, playing with those flags and coins in our living room. My dad asked me what currencies I was using and what my favorite flags and countries were.

I continued to play without looking at him, quickly saying with excitement, "I love the USA and playing the most with US dollars," even though it was obvious to my parents that the USA was my favorite, since the paper money was already worn-out, wrinkled, and a little dirty from my chocolate fingers, and God knows what else. My dad asked me, "How many dollars do you have then?" I stopped, and looked at him with a serious look, and asked, "Dad, how much is infinity?"

My dad smiled and exchanged a deep gaze with my mom, which I could not fully understand until many years letter. His answer was, "Bela, infinity is infinity, it can't be counted, there is always another number after the last number."

A few moments passed, and I broke the silence with, "One day I will count an endless amount of dollars" and continued playing.

I vividly remember other special times with my dad, lying down on the couch with my head on his lap while he was stroking my wild black curly hair during our movie marathons. These were black and white movies that we would watch over time together. Mahatma: Life of Gandhi, 1869-1948, one of our favorites, was five and a half hours long. I was so mesmerized by Gandhi, his life, and his people.

My brother and sister opted for other fun activities while giving me an opportunity to feel like a princess by having my dad all to myself so that I could ask him millions of questions. It was fascinating to learn about other peoples' culture, music, language, and food while watching the movies. While watching the Gandhi movie, I continually wondered why people wore different clothing, ate food with their hands, followed Gandhi, and came to his funeral.

I remember crying and feeling so sad, it was my first memory of someone dying, other than the big fish my mom got once from the market that was still breathing so we put it in water and kept feeding it until it mysteriously disappeared and "some other fish" ended up on our dinner table.

My dad's profound explanations laid the foundation of the true meaning of leadership and the types of leadership, which I have taken to heart ever since.

There was not much difference in how my loving grandma Angela also taught me about leadership and how she helped me each year to send my small donations to Mother Theresa's charity that at that time operated in Africa. I was ecstatic to get postcards or letters about the kids that my donation assisted in small villages. What fascinated me the most were the photos of kids with big smiles who looked so different than me or anyone I knew at that time. I wondered why and how their skin was so dark; it must be because of the sun I thought.

My undying hunger for knowledge and curiosity continued as I consumed every page of the World Encyclopedias and history books that I could get my hands on. I was very lucky to have an older brother and sister who shared their knowledge and a nice sized home library where I could access many books. I quickly advanced with my reading and writing on a wide range of topics in our home through books. I did not know how lucky I was until later in life. My parents were relieved to be able to allow me to find my answers instead of bugging them with millions of questions on a daily basis. I was Curious George on steroids growing up.

I started my first day of "real" school as a six year old, refusing to stay a day longer in preschool and fully ready to take on the new, endless opportunities presented to my limitless creative mind. I already knew by then how to read and write the Latin alphabet and I was eager to start learning the Cyrillic one.

Thanks to Olga, my wonderfully patient first-grade teacher, new friends, and books, my world instantly grew bigger.

It was 1980. Watching the opening ceremonies of the Winter Olympic Games had me yearning to explore this world. I had followed the travel of the Olympic torch from Ancient Olympia all the way to Lake Placid, New York. The torch was in the country that I daydreamed about often, with the promise of one day fully exploring – the United States of America!

I could not wait to ask in class about the true meaning behind the torch, the flame, and its travel. I loved the story about the land of Greek gods and goddesses. But this time history was unfolding in front of my eyes with many unexpected twists and turns.

My eyes got bigger and my smile wider as I was securing my spot, "my first position" as I called it, in the front of the TV. I was glued to the Olympics programming, hanging on to every word that was shared, intuitively picking and choosing the countries and Olympians I wanted to win. I could feel something bigger than anything else I had experienced before – The Olympic spirit! It was all about participation in the world's competition, the best of the best.

In the moments of my complete obsession with the Olympic Games, athletes, flags, languages, and people, I proclaimed yet another shocking thing to my family. "Dad, I want to be Olympian!" My brother looked at me as if had ten heads and laughed. Dad just smiled and asked, "What sport, Bela?"

"Skier. No, ski jumper or skater... anything dad!" My voice was full of excitement as it echoed in our living room. Seconds later my brother ruined my joy by saying, "Don't you see that boys are Olympians? You have to be as strong as a boy, and fast, and really good to be an Olympian."

As I stared at the TV, paying close attention, I noticed that mostly men were competing, and very few women were represented and only in select sports like figure skating.

"Why is that?" I wondered "Is it truly because the boys are stronger or better? What was wrong with the girls?" In my world, I was able to do everything perfectly fine amongst my friends who were the same age and even older.

I just could not understand why more boys were Olympians than girls and why girls were not allowed to do the same things, such as ski jumping or playing ice hockey. I felt like I could be a perfect jumper since I was small and light, and I thought it would be super cool to fly. Ski jumping looked to me like something I could do easily on grandpa's ranch, with all the downhill slopes waiting for me.

My dad explained swiftly, "It is a man's sport sweetheart, it is too dangerous for girls." I instantly asked him, "Like football too?" in reference to soccer. Soccer was my dad's and my favorite game. Mine mostly because I could watch long games with my dad and use it as an excellent opportunity to ask him questions while he would comment on the players' performances. I discovered later that my dad once was a very good player with a lot of potential to be a pro, but he was asked by his parents to finish college to be a mining engineer and forced to leave his big dream behind.

In his era, there was not much money to be spent on investing in player development or scholarships. During my youth, it was not much different either. If you were a boy and were really good, maybe you got a chance to play on decent teams and one day hopefully even on a professional team.

It was amazing to me to hear the TV anchor comment about someone's readiness, preparedness, poor pass, time out, or red or yellow card. I loved imitating this crazy football language that I knew inside out, but of course under my breath so my dad would not get upset.

I learned to predict who would win the game, totally depending on my instincts, and surprisingly to my dad's amusement, I was so often right. When his favorite "Hajduk" aka "the blue boys" would play, I had to be very careful when telling him my prognosis of the game. I learned early on that no matter how much you love specific players and an overall team, they just can't win all the time. Losing was part of the game too; the only difference was the true reason behind it. Was it poor teamwork, or coaching, or an individual player underperforming?

Determined that I still wanted to be an Olympian, even after the end of the 1980 Winter Olympic Games, I came up with yet another brilliant idea that was inspired by the book, "Under the Rainbow." It was about a boy who wanted to be a girl. I could not understand why he would want to do that. To change his gender, he needed to run under a rainbow. So my plan was to wait until spring and to chase rainbows until that happened. I wanted to be a boy so badly. I was playing all the time with boys, so I thought I might as well be one.

My playtime with boys was very adventurous, collaborative, and drama free. Plus we were very physically active. I did not care if I got hurt, bruised, cut, or dirty. I felt most free and fearless while playing with the boys, enjoying my life to fullest.

I loved playing football, playing chess, playing with my currency kit, and more than anything just playing with the boys. So in my little six year old head, it made perfect sense to be a boy. I even wanted to dress as a boy as much as possible, unless I was forced to wear a skirt and shiny girly shoes to church. I felt so funny doing that. I was a tall, twiggy, skinny kid, so my dad affectionately called me Olivia as in "Olive Oyl," the wife of the popular Popeye cartoon character.

As you can imagine, running under a rainbow never worked for me, so I had to learn to cope in other ways to be an athlete or Olympian stuck in a girl's body.

Somehow, deep down I knew that it would be "mission impossible," and that I was ready to explore further this new path for me.

That following winter I took on another challenge. I learned how to ski downhill on my own without knowing how to stop, never thinking for a second about it. My first crash resulted in a big bump on my head and black and blue bruises on my legs, but I was ready to do it again. The crash did not stop me; I just learned that there is more to skiing than going fast down a hill.

I was getting ready for the next big winter Olympic Games. I felt like the whole world was also getting ready with me since they were happening literally in my world – Sarajevo, Bosnia and Herzegovina, the heart of Yugoslavia.

The joy that I felt for the whole world to come to us was priceless. I could not stop talking about it for months. My questions about the sports and events got more complex and longer, as my brother and sister started to tease me, clearly annoyed by my demands to watch sports instead of movies. I was excited to watch downhill races, bobsledding, ice-skating, hockey, and so much more.

As I was glued to the television every free moment I had, I was fascinated by the new languages I kept hearing, yet another dimension that was added to my fascination with the world map, currencies, and flags. Some of the languages I heard sounded funny, some harsh or simply different, and some of them so melodic and appealing. Deep down, I wished that I could understand them all, or better yet speak them all.

After attending the 1984 Olympic Games, I felt an undying hunger to travel the world. I could not wait any longer for summer break and our family trip to the Adriatic coast. Although I still had to wait to travel internationally, I was able to indulge in weekend trips in different parts of what was then still one country called Yugoslavia on the weekends with my grandparents.

I was lucky that I had my guardian angel by my side, my grandma Angela, and my grandpa to go on road trips to visit family members.

On the road trips, I would be quiet in the back seat, always ready for a new adventure. I would gaze at the scenery and get excited that I would soon be at a new destination that I could explore. I was so happy that my world started getting bigger, excited to find new places on the road map with symbols of tunnels, a legend of many types of roads, lists of cities, and more. I was fascinated by how everything was so precisely measured, and loved answering questions like "If we are going 55 kilometers per hour, and our trip is 255 km, when will we arrive at such and such place?"

I continued to yearn for the world in which I could be an Olympian, learn a new language, travel, and see other people from remote parts of the world, like during the Olympics in Sarajevo.

As we know, our childhood dreams do not go exactly the way we want, regardless of how much spinach we eat in our attempts to be as strong as Popeye. Some of us always stayed like Olive Oyl. No matter what we would do or how hard we would play with the boys, we would not be good enough to play soccer on a professional team or be an Olympian.

While my childhood dream of being an Olympian was not to be realized, nor were the associated dreams of being a football player or a tennis player, my journey would frame a new dream: my desire to be an educator, teaching history or geography, or both, rooted in my love of sports and travel.

Many years later, I would understand what I was looking for – to understand what the Olympic spirit is and to help others discover their "Olympic" dream.

Today, by looking at the scars on my knees and elbows, I can't help but smile at the most memorable moments of my childhood. My scars were my trophies!

The other happiest moments in my life, of my childhood, that I deeply cherish were when I was blazing through elementary school, fully immersed in history and geography. A deep desire to be an educator emerged since I could not be an Olympian or even a professional football player despite my love for the game.

I lived in an era where not much was invested in women's sports. Monica Seles was very lucky I thought, her dad was her coach, and he was okay that she was a girl. I fell in love with tennis, following Monica's playing as much as I could, hoping that one day I may be a professional tennis player. Soon I learned that in specialized sports, like tennis, you had to start playing very early and that it required special training, equipment, coaches, money, time, and so much practice. I felt like I was out of luck again.

I learned through my numerous conversations with professional athletes and coaches that one key factor to success is family and their support. For instance, Monica had a very supportive dad who got her going to play tennis when she was only five years old. Interestingly, her mom and grandma thought that a girl should not spend so much time playing tennis.

Luckily, she sided with her dad and continued to practice until she reached the number one junior tennis player status in the world by the age of thirteen. Later, I could not be prouder of her when she reached the world's number one ranking at only seventeen years of age! I felt in a way that this was my victory too as well as all girls around the world who were told that they are not good enough or that professional sports are only for boys.

The presence of the family or lack of it can go both ways, and it can cut deep wounds if you grow up in broken families and were challenged by many difficult situations. This can hinder a young athlete's success, due to a lack of confidence, support, and overall family support and understanding.

The replacement for that support for many athletes are coaches, teachers, and substitute families. In some cases, social service workers, churches, or parents of other kids in school fill this role.

So many of us are taught that we should not make mistakes growing up, as a result we would not even want to do something new. In fact, there is nothing wrong with making a mistake. It is all about what you say and do after you mess up that truly matters. How you "self-talk" and behave can be a big game changer in your overall performance or lack of it. I keep hearing due to fears and self-doubt that many of us will never give ourselves permission to try even.

How sad, lonely, and dark that place can be – especially if you grow up in a culture that can be so harsh, open, and direct, with people who have lots of opinions, prejudice, and judgment. It can make you weaker or even break you or make you stronger and better. In my case, it broke me a couple of times but made me stronger for a marathon – a life long journey I never dreamed would happen.

The best part is each one of us has a choice for action or non-action, for staying in fear or stepping out of fear. There is nothing wrong with failing in life after trying hard. But it is wrong in my opinion if you failed without giving it your best shot, or best shots for a given opportunities, regardless of what they may be. Why?

I learned to abandon my fears after a while and face problems head on. Especially while growing up with an older brother and sister. Quickly I learned that for me, being shy and reserved would not get me far. As I started to make more friends in school, I discovered that to be the case in "the real world" too. For me, this was a new skill that enabled a new me to be ready to conquer the world.

It made me not only survive but also thrive while living in five different countries on my own. It saved my life more than ten times. On this astonishing life path, many years later, I understood what I was looking for – to discover the true spirit of an Olympian.

Take Action:

Discovering or Reconnecting With Your Dream

I invite you to consider discovering and reconnecting with your dream(s) by thinking about and answering these questions as a guide to achieving them.

1. What is your dream(s)?

2. What are you doing to achieve your dream(s)? Who is supporting you in your pursuit?

3. What is stopping you from reaching your dream(s)? Do you need to reframe your dream(s)?

Chapter Two

Finding Your Own "Olympic" Spirit

"The most important thing in the Olympic Games is not to win but to take part, just as the most important thing in life is not the triumph but the struggle. The essential thing is not to have conquered but to have fought well." ~ **Olympic Spirit**

As I was in search of my Olympic dream growing up in the former Yugoslavia, I yearned to find the true Olympic spirit. That discovery came later in my life, in the most profound way through meeting and befriending a Pakistani Olympian in field hockey, Imran Warsi. A handsome Iranian whose big smile can fill a room, he is also a photo model, actor, and poet.

I enjoyed numerous conversations with him about his life and his beliefs on success. Through him, I discovered several profound, golden nuggets of wisdom.

For Imran, life is living every day in faith. He sees it as a very simple process though it often gets unnecessarily overly complicated. Every day he shoots for the stars and aims to reach the sky. Early in his life, he learned how to look at failure in a healthy way. Every time he would fail, he would see that as practice for a next better move until he reached his goal. He did not see failure as a punishment. He saw it as an amazing new opportunity. He acknowledges that he has made many mistakes, but he does not have many regrets because each mistake taught him something profound and deep.

What strikes me the most during our conversations is his sense of the past. "I am done with the past since I can't change it or do anything about it. On the other hand, the future has plenty of room for change." He does not want to use the past as an excuse to miss out on the future, especially the bright future that all of us are capable of creating. He had a very humble beginning; his first field hockey shoes were an old pair of shoes that he found in a secondhand store that a cobbler in town fixed for him to make them better fit his growing feet.

They were not even the right type of shoes for field hockey, but he did not want to use that as an excuse to not show up on the field and practice.

The fire in his belly and his goal-oriented mindset are his prized attributes. For him, "giving his best" and being the best he can be, is self-motivated, not based on pleasing his family, friends, coaches, or teammates.

Imran consciously makes every decision by putting God at the center of his life. Even if you are not religious, as many people are not, we may want to agree that something bigger and greater exists outside ourselves that keeps us going when all hope seems to be lost.

"Even when I fail, I never lose hope, because I know it could still happen." ~ Imran Warsi

A key role model when Imran was a very young child was his father, Ehtisham Warsi – also a noted field hockey athlete who played for the Pakistani National team.

When he spoke of his father, you could hear in his voice deep gratitude, respect, and love. I immediately connected with him and his story. Ehtisham was his mentor, coach, and his best friend. He recalls 5 AM mornings when his father would drag him to the field to play and teach him field hockey. He never listened to Imran's complaints; he just kept going. His father taught him something profound during those early days:

"Your biggest opponent is the one facing you in the mirror."
~ Ehtisham Warsi

Quickly he learned from his father that it is not going to be very easy to achieve everything in the profession of an athlete unless you strongly believe in yourself. And only then, when you truly do, do you have the power to change your destiny. Today, he plays in Kazan, Russia as a defender and penalty corner specialist for Dinamo Kazan.

Imran also immersed himself into his dreams so deeply with his end goal in mind – to be the best he can be, because his best will count the most when and where needed.

*"I always believe in working hard in silence while letting success make all the noise." ~ **Imran Warsi***

Deep down Imran knew early on that he was so lucky to have support and love as core ingredients to his success. He also knew in real life there are many other very talented players as well, perhaps better than him – but when he finally got the opportunity to play, he was ready. Why? He practiced every single day with anticipation of that opportunity. What happened next is history. Imran became a huge superstar!

When you ask Imran what was the key to his success, he will tell you humbly his parents and all of the people that truly love him. They have been his biggest blessing in life. Every day he talks to and influences young players by telling them to make their parents proud. In Imran's mind that is the most direct connection to God because God never refuses a parent's prayer.

*"**God never refuses a parent's prayer." ~ **Imran Warsi***

Our conversations also revealed a painful self-realization. Despite the success and a very prominent lifestyle with numerous opportunities outside of the field, such as photo modeling, acting, dancing, and parties, Imran feels a deep disconnect with the people around him.

People are busy more than ever, preoccupied so much with themselves, not having time for things that truly matter, such as basic human connection and conversation. I could not agree more.

> *Live life with a passion, because without*
> *passion life is nothing.*
> *Listen to your heart, because you can change*
> *the world if you listen with your heart.*
> *And when you do, then you can start*
> *reshaping the World*
> *The past is the missed opportunity,*
> *The present gives us the opportunity to*
> *plant the seeds,*
> *The future gives us the opportunity to*
> *cultivate love, respect, and kindness.*
> *Let us strive to spread happiness because*
> *happiness is in our heart, not circumstances!*
> **~ Imran Warsi**

Whoever is waiting for the perfect reason or perfect time to change is missing out! Why wait? Why fear? Sometimes we must dare to jump!

> *"I believe that we are all born with the ability to change*
> *someone's life."* **~ Imran Warsi**

Tears rolled down my face as I reflected on these many simple truths that cut so deep, first through our hearts and then penetrating our souls. At that moment, I sensed something very profound that took me years to figure out: Too many people in this world need to be taught kindness, compassion, and humility. I assumed that all of us had that within us. But the reality was different and rather frightening.

> *"Too many people in this world need to be taught kindness,*
> *compassion, and humility."* **~ Izabela, The World Messenger**

Unlike Imran's supportive childhood, Lars Lynge, a former independent Olympic Danish downhill skier, had a very different experience. Lars' Olympic dream was very real, so real that he almost lost his life. As I was sitting in a coffee shop in Denver, I could not stop smiling. What were the odds of running into Lars here in Denver as I was writing this book about something that instantly connected us – the Winter Olympic Games in 1984 in Sarajevo, Bosnia and Herzegovina?

Lars' father, a Danish sailing Olympian, was very harsh and disapproving of Lars, his only child. Early in Lars' life, and while he was growing up, painfully and sadly his father's Olympic spirit never reflected in a positive way while raising his only son. It was painful for Lars to deal with his dad's harshness, disapproval, and negativity to the point that he learned to cope with his dad's bitterness and put downs in a way that would minimize and neutralize the conflict—yet still leave a big void in his life for his dad's approval, support, and love.

For a little boy to be told over and over that he is nothing, cuts so deep. Just listening to his story made me sad, wondering what kind of upbringing his dad had to have so that he would behave in such a horrible way. Why do adults opt to have a child when they are unwilling to raise them the correct way – with love, support, and compassion? Sadly, I have seen so much pain in the eyes of so many adults as well as kids as a result of their painful upbringing. I wonder when and how this cycle will break and hopefully fully stop and then change for the better.

It was heartbreaking to not have support at home when he needed it, let alone the opportunity to celebrate his success when it started coming as Lars started progressing with his first sport: sailing dinghies. Lars got the support and optimism that he needed to find his purpose and a positive outlet through worldwide sailing classes. He got his technique down, but he had the worst and cheapest dinghy to compete with, so for a while Lars was always last.

He was so happy that he could compete and participate, never letting his poor results affect his spirit to give up or his drive to not try just a little harder the next day. He did not know the difference. He never thought it was because of a dinghy; he initially thought it was because of him until a breakthrough occurred. He got an opportunity through his Boy Scout sailing club to receive a new dinghy. The first time Lars sailed a brand new dinghy, he finished the race first.

From then on, he was always first, consistently winning for two years. His dad never, not even once, came to see him race even during these two years of consistent wins. He never congratulated him or asked him questions about his day at school or the race successes that he had. Since Lars could not talk or celebrate at home, the relationship between him and his dad remained underdeveloped. Lars achieved an amateur, professional status as a sailor at the age of 12.

After that, Lars ventured into his other passion, downhill skiing. He was going through the Olympic program from 1980 in preparation for the 1984 winter Olympics in Sarajevo. The program that he was part of was not good, and the competition was too high – 12 people in the program competing for four spots only. At that time, he did not have much support or resources, so he decided to make his own team. He eventually got sponsors and very much needed support, but he was still missing a good program and team to train with on a regular basis.

He got on the Russian Olympic team to train and practice with during the most intense political times—the era of an active Russian Secret Police and political shifts in Europe as well as other parts of the world. At that time, Lars did not know what he was getting himself into until he found himself in the middle of nowhere practicing with a hard core Russian trainer that did everything under the sun to make "Mother Russia proud" at the next Olympic competition.

Lars trained with them for three painful years in a strenuous boot camp, the type of training he never saw anywhere else. The fear factor was high on a daily basis. He learned how to endure all of it, including the stone cold faces of the coaches who would infuse more fear and pressure through their shouting or yelling.

What Lars learned is that you can be the best in any sport. But to compete in the Olympics, it limits you more than you can imagine. The level of effort, training, preparation, and constant pressure needed during the Olympiad time, the four-year period between the Olympic Games, was mentally, emotionally, and physically challenging. He had to beat the best of the best to qualify event to go, still with no guarantee of competing in the Games. He had to give up many social aspects of his life that his friends were able to enjoy.

The mental and emotional challenge that you experience during this time of the "unknown" can affect the most brilliant athletes. You are lucky if you do not get a physical injury since you push yourself every day a little bit further and train a little bit harder, without knowing what the rest of the competition is doing or looks like. There are no mercy or excuses.

"It does not matter if a coach or trainer, mom or dad tells you 'You can do it,' it matters if YOU think you can do it!" ~ **Lars Lange**

The key to success as an athlete, especially as an Olympian, is if you think you can do what it takes to succeed. There was an instant mutual respect and shared understanding of what it takes to survive and then thrive between us since we both took some very bold action against all odds and we succeeded in the end. Lars learned to be a change agent and to change his attitude as needed to cope in the best way with stress, expectations, and high competition.

When he finally got a chance to ski in Sarajevo in a pre-qualifying race against other skiers, he felt ready. He was lucky to be sponsored by Rossignol with skiing equipment. That day, the Olympic

Mountains got some new snow on them. He was competing fourth in his first race. At that time, there was no instant communication or feedback to tell you who finished the race when, as you were waiting in line. The first three skiers all got disqualified as they missed turns due to unexpected icy conditions on the slopes or due to falling.

When it was Lars' turn to ski, he had an excellent start but he hit the ice with such high speed that he lost control and fell, breaking his neck. As you can imagine, at that moment all the years of hard work were taken away in one second. In fact, he almost lost his life. He was immediately flown to Innsbruck in Austria where he spent the next three months recovering, before starting physical therapy. He was diagnosed with partial neck paralyzes, which he refused to accept as a permanent disability. You have got to love his attitude and drive.

He worked hard through his process of rehabilitation, seeking alternative healing that he found in acupuncture and holistic healing. It took him years to fully rehabilitate, but in the end he regained over 95% of the movement in his neck.

As you can guess, due to his injury, he was not able to compete again and never got the chance to qualify in another Olympic competition. But what he has done since then is remarkable.

He re-invented himself! Lars learned to think and act differently based on the current conditions of the situation he was in. He learned how to separate himself from the crowd and be successful in other aspects of his life. He became a successful TV sports commentator and covered events and activities at the Olympics. He became one of the first specialized sporting goods high-end brand owners, offering skiers and snowboarders the best quality products.

But his undying Olympic spirit and need to satisfy his adrenalin rush, in addition to his need to do something bold again, to stand, to be better than average, and to be better than the best, propelled him to do something different and new. Lars is a pioneer in paragliding in Europe!

He was the first and only one to do that, before an official name for the adventure sport was even implemented. He had the first custom-made lightweight glider that allowed him to see and to appreciate the world in a very new way. Some people are just meant to soar with eagles.

Years later, paragliding regulations and requirements were implemented in Europe, then in the US, and then in other parts of the world.

The key lesson to be learned is this: If what you want, wish, or desire can't happen exactly the way you want, you can always re-define your goal or objective and find a way for it to happen! Some call it plan B. It does not mean it is a less worthy choice or accomplishment. It can, in fact, be more rewarding than you ever thought it could be.

Take Action:

Finding Your Own "Olympic" Spirit

I invite you to ponder what an "Olympic" spirit means to you through these set of questions.

Note: If you don't admire an athlete, that's OK, substitute another role (perhaps a Community Leader, Statesperson or Business Leader) for these questions.

1. Who is your favorite Olympian? What qualities do they have that you admire?

2. What steps can you take to achieve these qualities?

3. What is holding you back?

Chapter Three

Acknowledging Your Breaking Point

Right before I turned 16, a boy expressed interest in me who was at least six or seven years older. Many of the boys in former Yugoslavia would not take no for an answer in their romantic pursuits or in life in general, even when I would kindly decline to do things with them, like going to the movies, going to a cafe after school, or taking a walk with them to the park. Some of them would be persistent until they would "score" a yes. For older boys this was like a game, the only difference was that the rules could change at any given time. The outcome was unfortunately often too painful for many "boy players" and girls.

As more harassment occurred during short breaks between my late afternoon classes or outside of my high school, I was thinking about how to find a peaceful and "ladylike" solution to the problem since I was reaching a breaking point. Should I tell my older brother, who was a very tall and strong basketball player? No, this was not a good idea. He could hurt them or get hurt. After all, I only had one brother. My dad? Nope! It would create more problems.

I would probably be asked to come home before sunset. Not taking any chances on that one. I was frustrated that this had become my issue. I wondered why I should have to take responsibility for someone else's poor behavior. Why couldn't people just take responsibility for their own actions? Sadly, that was a question that kept reoccurring even in my adult life.

As a creative teen at that time, I found a fun, yet great solution one day on my walk home. The next day, I decided to wear my skinny jeans tucked into my soft leather boots and my dad's vest from one of his Italian suits that I could perfectly fit to my girl's body with a black top underneath. With a big smile, I added my brother's precious piece of property from the time when we played cowboys, a sheriff's badge.

The badge was a shiny, cheap, sliver of metal with big "SHERIFF" letters in the middle. I put it on the vest right over my racing heart, and I immediately felt my Super Power.

I was ready at that moment to face anything and anyone without any fear. I felt like Wyatt Earp at the O.K. Corral ready to take down the bad guys all at once!

Walking to school that day, I felt taller and more powerful with a big smile on my face. That day and the rest of the week at school, kids looked at me, especially the boys, but they did not say anything, they just stared at me or avoided my intense gaze by looking down or sideways. Boys that used to push me around on the stairs so that they could accidentally touch me or grab me would move and look away as if I had ten heads or something. But no one would say a word.

My confidence level was at an all-time high until my last class on that Friday evening. On my way out, it was dark, and I instinctively knew that one of my harassers was there. I took a deep breath and started walking like a puma, ready to jump at any moment, fully prepared to act on my instincts. The books in my hands were very heavy with sharp corners, perfect for defense I thought. Also, the new mixed martial arts moves I had learned from my uncle the previous winter made me even more confident.

This time, to my amusement, I only got looks, and a comment under the breath of my harasser, "...wow, lucky us, we've got a new Sheriff in town," followed by the dumbest laughter I ever heard. I kept walking, tall and proud, without stopping or saying anything back. Several minutes later, he stopped following me. Before I knew it, I was at home and relieved that my plan had worked, and I had not been harassed by any of the boys, in particular, my most frequent harasser.

The next day, I had yet another brilliant plan that I just could not wait to put into action. Saturday morning was a day when everyone in town went to the local market to buy fresh produce from local farmers. There were always tons of people, chatter, and fun interactions everywhere.

After the market shopping was done, people would go to local cafés for an afternoon coffee, catching up with friends and family. That morning, me as "the new Sheriff in town" showed up in the midst of the chaos having fun, lots of fun.

As I was passing by, I saw my harasser with his mom, carrying her grocery bags. I stopped right in front of them, staring directly at him, and then I extended my greetings to his mom politely. I asked his mom if her son had something to say to me, since he was acting like mom's perfect boy. He was blushing and could not even look me in the eyes. His mom was confused. I told her that he is very loud and daring at other occasions and that I wanted to give him a chance to tell me whatever it was that he had on his mind for months now.

I smiled and offered him an opportunity to express himself. He was silent, looking down at his new All Star shoes, acting like a complete idiot. His mom was even more confused as she was looking one second at me and the other second at him. Politely I excused myself and wished them both a great weekend, and I left. I was skipping from pure joy on my way back home. Even today, when I walk my dog Jack, when I am so happy, I skip. In my mind, skipping does not have an age limit, and if you are looking for a skipping pass, then I am granting you one for a lifetime!

That afternoon, during our family dinner, my dad interrupted our family chatter with a blunt comment to my mom. *"Katarina, did you know that we have a new sheriff in town?"* My mom looked at him as if he were crazy or drunk. My older brother and sister quickly stood up from the table and rushed to the door leaving the dining room. I stood up ready to follow them when my dad's comment stopped me in my tracks. *"Olive Oyl, do you happen to know anything about that?"*

My reaction was *"About what dad?"* until he just looked at me and said seriously, *"Show me what you were wearing today!"* At that moment, I knew the game was over. I went to retrieve his vest with the Sheriff's badge and handed the items to him.

He was holding back his smile as he was trying to be serious while my mom was watching us with amusement. *"You took my vest?"* my dad declared seriously as if in shock. *"Yup, you were not wearing it anyway dad,"* I answered abruptly, without thinking strategically at that moment, very honestly, and a bit naïvely.

My dad looked at me while saying to my mom, *"Did you know that your daughter was a sheriff in town today?"* I was smiling, and I quickly answered, *"Dad, the sheriff was in town for the whole week, not only today!"* As soon as I blurted that, I felt bad, but I could not help it, I was programmed to say the truth regardless of what my punishment might be.

At that point, my lovely mom started laughing so loud and hard that I joined her as my dad was trying hard to keep a straight face. I was dismissed, while my siblings were in the living room watching TV, wondering why we were laughing so hard. My loving dad made it clear before I left, *"Bela, there is only one sheriff in the house!"* as I walked away, I knew that the sheriff wasn't me.

That night I smiled going to bed, feeling so good in so many ways. I felt free, liberated by facing my fear head on. The best part was that I found a solution to my problem on my own and I felt so proud. I felt fearless. I felt good about my actions.

"By facing fear you come to discover what is and what is not!"
~ Izabela, The World Messenger

That day I also learned something very profound. If you break some small rules for a bigger cause or purpose, it is okay as long as no harm is done to anyone. My dad's vest still looked the same, as did my brother's badge. My siblings in the end had a great laugh too. This was the moment when I understood fully what Lao Tzu meant years earlier. *"Being deeply loved by someone gives you strength, while loving someone deeply gives you courage."*

That day I felt a love from my father in his own way that gave me the strength to act on my own as I did. But the courage came from me, from my capacity to see things in a light, positive way, instead of with fear.

The next evening, as I was lying down underneath the clear sky with a scattering of glistening, majestic stars, I asked for miracles, many miracles, for the whole world to be showered with the miracles. And soon, as many miracles started to unfold in my life, I started to wonder how? Why? Why me? Why now?

As my long black curly hair was moved with a humming warm wind that night, I felt the announcement of a new beginning, the announcement of a big change coming my way. But little did I know what the change would be and how it would impact my life, other than the importance of following my gut instinct to find a creative way to address an issue before I reached a breaking point.

One profound symbolic change was that of the Holiday Inn hotel that was built in Sarajevo, Bosnia and Herzegovina to accommodate the athletes during the winter Olympic Games of 1984. It represented so much to the people of Sarajevo and former Yugoslavia, including its design, resembling brown and yellow Legos. As a nine year old kid, it was a super cool building.

Unfortunately during the Balkan civil war in the 1990s, it became symbolic of a hiding place and a refuge for local and foreign journalists reporting on the horrors of the brotherly blood bath that would last for over four years in the heart of Yugoslavia, in the heart of Europe. This was the most unspeakable conflict, terror, and war for me to witness and live through. For me, it was the most insane, primitive, unnecessary conflict at the end of the 20th century!

It was heartbreaking to think that someone who enjoyed trust in our community, even my trust, someone who went to church every Sunday, and taught kids to sing in a church choir, ended up being a perpetrator during the siege of Sarajevo and its neighboring towns.

Listening to my gut was instinctual for me even as a young child, before briefly becoming "the new Sheriff in town." Unlike me, my older sister Inga, a blond, green-eyed sweet girl wanted so badly to sing when we were young girls. I was not impressed at all with our choir teacher. My gut was right then, as it was years later during the war, that the true character of this man behind the composed authority figure was exposed.

I was a small, skinny, shy child in the background with shiny black hair and big dark eyes that would sing very softly at first, making it impossible to hear me. I was asked to project my voice louder, and I was constantly corrected. I felt frustrated, harassed, and honestly by then knew I was very musically challenged. I interjected my voice at the wrong time and with the wrong pitch. I was interfering with the angelic sound of the choir at St. Michael's Church with the magical piano sound in the background. While I liked the great music and sounds in church, these lessons gave me a lot of stress and with very little support or encouragement. I started to feel strong resentment toward the church.

I was dismissed from the church choir several weeks later as I had frustrated my piano teacher one too many times. Although I was relieved, I was deeply saddened to tell my parents that I didn't have the magical singing voice of my grandfather (my mom's dad), a religious fanatic, in my mind, who influenced my parents to be more active in church. Even back then I had my own very clearly defined roles of politics, religion, and education that could not seduce or manipulate me into acts of injustice in God's name, especially when too many people started to play God right before war broke out.

But a victory this time was truly bittersweet. Unfortunately, my sister was dismissed from the choir as well even though her voice was choir material. I guess the teacher just did not want to see either one of us anymore. My sister was devastated, and I felt so bad for her. I did not have any idea that it would affect her in the way that it did. This was when I realized that not everything always goes as planned.

Many years later through school and growing up in our community, I realized how many people judged you or labeled you based on their impressions of your siblings, their academic accomplishments, parents, grandparents, class, status, heritage, religion, ethnicity, you name it, that at the end of the day had very little to do with you – the real you.

Deep down, at that moment before I turned ten, I started to have a deep yearning to be judged based only on who I am as me, solely based on my actions and behaviors, my moral compass, and the outcomes I was able to generate. Not that my family was bad or that I was ashamed of them, but I felt that so many things where predetermined for me in my life before I was in the position to even make a choice. Everything in me was screaming, "Please give me a break!"

I am sure you can relate in some ways with what you went through during your own childhood. I bet you were not the only Izabela in your town as I was. My parents would come home after work, where they would hear the story of the day. Many times my name would get thrown into a story, even if I had nothing to do with it.

That Saturday morning when I was kicked out of church choir, I could not wait to share with my dad my remarkable day. When talking with my dad I told him, "I guess I may have more talents in playing football than in singing." He just smiled as my poor mom was wondering when I would start acting like a girl as I rushed to my room to get out of my skirt and shiny shoes. I was on a mission to put on my favorite sneakers, shorts, and a t-shirt so that I could play with my favorite friends, the boys in my neighborhood. My dad just kept smiling as he could read through my deep sense of relief that came too quickly over my face as I was rushing out to door to catch up on my playtime.

My sister, however, was not happy for weeks, blaming me for her getting kicked out of the choir. In retrospect, I am so grateful that my sister did not spend much time with the choir teacher whom I never trusted, even though people commented that he was "a nice role model within the community." My gut would cringe when I heard those or similar words.

Luckily, that summer my sister found a new hobby, writing poetry, something that she was quite good at and enjoyed doing. She especially enjoyed it after being diagnosed with type one diabetes and struggling to find ways to adjust to her new life as a diabetic. It was not easy, despite my mom's medical background, because there was not much information and research about type one diabetes in children in comparison to adults. Initially, she was told that she couldn't play sports and be active.

Overnight, I became the Older Sister, even though she was a year and a half older. I watched her like a hawk, making sure that she could adjust to her new condition in the best way possible. It was a big game changer for everyone in our family, especially for my sister. It would also prepare me for what we would endure as we escaped later in life.

During the time that I was a high school student, I realized that my goal of becoming an Olympian was not meant to be. Despite my passion and athleticism, a painful inflammation of my wrists prevented me from playing basketball or any other sport that required me to use my hands. Instead, I enrolled in dancing school and by the time I graduated from high school, I was able to dance extremely well in anything from classic to modern dances, making my mom proud that I had finally transformed from the young tomboy that I had been growing up into a young lady. I loved ballroom dancing, but my favorites were the fast and exotic moves like the Rumba, Argentine Tango, Cha-Cha, Rock and Roll, and of course, Disco.

This was a critical moment in my life because when one dream died, another was born. My new dream was to go to college and become an educator and to influence kids, which I did. Part of my upbringing in socialistic Yugoslavia was to take high school trips, excursions to a wide range of European countries. Many trips were great, and I enjoyed them very much.

Some were important but not pleasant, such as the trip to the Auschwitz concentration camp in Poland, which was heartbreaking. As a young teenager, I found myself standing in the middle of the camp weeping like a baby. Thoughts of the old black and white documentaries that they showed us in a school filled my head but did not compare to what I saw with my own eyes. I personally saw rooms full of human hair, shoes, clothing, prosthetics, battered suitcases, and the gas chambers and incinerators overflowing with burnt skeletons of men, women, and children. It was unspeakable.

This was the first time that I could smell, touch, feel, and hear the echo of the worst kinds of fear. As I was standing in the middle of the concentration camp, I looked up at a gray cloudy sky and proclaimed, "I will do everything I can to never, never allow this to happen again" as tears continued to roll down my cheeks. From that moment on, I had an even deeper yearning to make the world a better place for new generations.

In a million years, I could not have possibly imagined that this excursion would prepare me, in its own mysterious way, to not only survive the horrors of the Balkan war and the horrific genocide, but to also be strong enough to help others get through it too.

This Balkan war did not begin with an invasion from another country as did other wars begun many times throughout the centuries. Instead, it came from an invasion within. Those who were once our neighbors, friends, teachers, community leaders, and even family members became enemies.

One day, early in the morning, I received a call from my friend Natasha from Belgrade. As soon I answered, she asked me abruptly: "Who is killing all those people?" and before I could say a word I heard static noise, and then our call was abruptly disconnected.

I was never able to reconnect with her gain. I was puzzled at first, then more and more concerned.

Before we knew it, Yugoslavia was split and morphed into a war zone that spread hatred, chaos, and fear. I began to feel a heightened state of apprehension because I knew something was not right. Shortly after Natasha's call, I watched the news and began to understand that a nationalistic uprising was unfolding.

The more I thought about my call with Natasha, the more I felt that she had been trying to warn me about the pending storm that was heading my way. When I shared my thoughts with my family, they said that everything was fine. Even one of my uncles, who was a National Security Agent in an organization in the former Yugoslavia roughly similar to the Federal Bureau of Investigation (FBI), dismissed the possibility of conflicts in Bosnia and Herzegovina. No one believed that it could happen.

My other uncle, who was a successful young lawyer in Sarajevo, was also skeptical that the conflicts we had started to see unfolding in Croatia would flair up to that level in Bosnia and Herzegovina.

At this time, Sarajevo was the most multi-ethnic, cosmopolitan city in the country, and it was unimaginable that neighbor would turn on a neighbor in this region.

It was the fall of 1990 when the nationalistic uprising began. War was officially declared the following spring in 1991. Luckily my brother, a third year law school student and a very talented college basketball player at the time, managed to escape right before a major blood bath occurred in the heart of Yugoslavia, Sarajevo, and its surroundings. The rest of my family was not as fortunate.

My father and older sister were both diabetic and began to develop severe complications from the disease. My mother, a medical nurse, was preoccupied with helping others in their never-ending need.

And my younger sister needed help navigating the constant disruptions in her elementary education. During the day, I'd take care of my family while I was studying to be an elementary school teacher, and at night I volunteered with the Red Cross helping refugees. It wasn't long before I found myself becoming emotionally and physically numb.

> *"Nothing can be as rewarding as serving others during their greatest need."* ~ **Izabela, The World Messenger**

My world was shattered when I was "asked" by the ruling party in a town outside of Sarajevo to use my speaking skills to spread propaganda news on a local TV station and one of the hundreds of radio stations that popped up during the war. The mission was to spread more fear, hate, and propaganda to ordinary people seen as "casualties of the war."

When I refused, I was told that the next time my answer would be very different. The perpetrators knew that my father was slowly dying from diabetic complications and urgently needed care beyond what was offered in a town with limited electricity, insulin, and healthcare. My love for my dad was beyond any measure. I knew that by doing what I was told, I could help keep him alive.

But at what cost to hundreds if not thousands of other innocent people that I cared so much for? There were no easy answers and I began to taste the worst type of fear. I became restless and couldn't sleep more than four hours a night.

I was afraid they would come back and do something horrible to my family, which they did. This time they came in the middle of the day to our family store where I worked while helping so many local people and refugees in town. I recognized one of them. He was a former martial arts instructor and someone who I had called a friend. They leered at me with evil smiles.

This time, I was not only pressured to spread propaganda, but I was also asked to "entertain" local and foreign military leaders. Several local restaurants and a hotel outside of town in the woods were used for the entertainment. I was invited to join "the event" at the local restaurant as a special guest where alcohol, food, and drugs were in endless supply, in addition to other offerings.

Somehow, I stood, and without an ounce of fear, thanked them for coming and asked them to leave our store. At that moment I knew I would have to fight them, not with force because this would be a very short game with only one winner, who would not be me. Instead, I had to act boldly, courageously, and fearlessly if we were to survive.

A week later, just hours before sunrise on my way home from working for the Red Cross at the local high school, where I served refugees in need of warm milk and food, I sensed danger as I crossed a bridge five minutes from the relative safety of my home. At first, all I could see was the burning tip of a cigarette. Then a cold voice from the dark asked me, "Where do you think you are going?" I stopped for a second and quickly responded, "Home."

Stepping out from the shadows, he smiled while he pulled his pistol and aimed it at my head. His hand was shaking while he was loudly laughing. He was obviously drunk, and his eyes were empty.

Although I clearly recognized the danger, I somehow stayed calm. Everything slowed down, including my breathing.

Momentarily, I froze. Is this real? Where can I hide? Can I jump? Run? Where will protection come from? Is this my ending? Will I ever again see my loved ones?

As I processed my limited options, a voice in the dark suddenly yelled, "Leave her alone! She is one of us, you idiot. Do you even know who she is?"

A few seconds later the gun disappeared into his holster, and he staggered away laughing like a crazy man.

The familiar, friendly voice in the dark came from a man who I kindly turned down numerous times in romantic pursuits during my high school years. It shocked me that he was sticking his neck out for me like that.

What happened next surprised me even more. He walked me home in complete silence until we reached my building.

He looked around, pulled me close, and whispered in my ear, "Bela, it is getting more and more dangerous around here. If you can, find a way to get out. I may not be able to help you next time."

His pleading eyes reflected the seriousness of his every word. Before I could say anything, he kissed me on my lips and disappeared into the dark. The last time I saw him was at my dad's funeral when he gave me a hug and a kiss on my cheeks.

My world started to collapse in slow motion, more and more each day. I felt like I was falling apart as well. But I knew that if I lost my focus and strength at those moments, it would not only be the end of me but also of my loved ones. Instinctively I felt more and more fearless as more danger was rising.

During my dad's last 45 days of life, I slept very little. I was restless and confused. What saved me from my inner demons was what I later understood to be emotional intelligence. In the last precious moments before he died, my father weakly whispered: *"Never sell your soul to the devil. He will be back and will always ask for more until there is nothing else left to give."*

His deep love for me reflected the most profound message of all time: the importance of doing the right thing no matter what we may face, without losing our own values and integrity, even at great personal cost.

He gave me a new task, something worth living for. During one of our last conversations, he said, "You can't save me; my days are numbered. Let me die in peace. But you must save your diabetic sister because she will not last much longer if she stays here in this war zone. That is your mission, Bela."

As he was gasping for air, I knelt by his side. His kidneys were failing, his body was holding more and more water, and his breathing was weaker. As I looked at him with deep unconditional love and sorrow, with a weak smile I held back my tears. I felt so defeated and helpless. But my dad's wisdom and strength emboldened me, and it gave me a renewed purpose and fearless determination.

"I will fulfill his final wish to save my diabetic sister," said a loud voice that kept coming back every time I would get caught in emotions of defeat, sadness, and sorrow. I kept thinking how I would make this happen since my sister did not even want to hear about the possibility of leaving home and our loved ones. With the support of my uncles, a master plan was created.

A few weeks later we escaped on the last convoy out from outside of Sarajevo to Croatia, where we hoped to continue our journey to Sweden, our place of safety.

It was once again bittersweet though because I had to hide, without disclosing my name on the passenger list.

There were many dangers for me, but I was specifically running away from the man who came to my family store and asked me to spread propaganda. And he was the one approving the final list of names allowed to leave the city.

Luckily my father's cousin ensured two spots on one of five buses heading out by listing my sister's name plus an "unnamed guardian." Later I found that my father's cousin was executed with a gunshot to the back of his head. When I learned of his murder, I felt that I was directly responsible for his death.

He was a good man, and it was so hard even to this day to understand the actions of pure insanity.

Our first five days on a journey that would, under "normal" circumstances, take just five to six hours began on winding back roads with fighting all around us. Our bus was full of old, sick, and wounded people. Besides a newly born baby with a young mother, I was the youngest. The very first day – in the sour mix of old urine, sweat, tears, and bodily waste – I detected another tangible stench, the smell of fear.

This time, the fear was so real that I would try to get relief by imagining in my head that I was going on one of my high school excursions, refusing to get drowned in the bottomless pit of human misery and pain.

"Life can test you by a new meaning of patience through self-discovery not by actual waiting, but by your behavior while you are waiting." ~ Izabela, The World Messenger

People were dead silent, almost paralyzed, and afraid to say or do anything. My sister's legs and feet started to swell to the point where she could not wear her shoes. Our food and water supply was almost gone. I stopped eating by the second day on the bus, saving everything for my sister since it was not clear when we would get to the next safe place to rest, eat, or even use the bathroom. I prayed to God to help me to find strength so I could be fearless and a rock for my sister.

Her insulin was almost depleted, and I was so worried that she might go into a diabetic coma at any moment. I was holding a small pack of sugar in my hand from the local café typically served with Bosnian coffee, as my only first aid help.

During the journey, we had to hide in the woods for some time with the engines of the buses turned off and wait until dark so that we didn't get bombed or picked up by patrols.

These were also limited opportunities to use the bathroom, without wandering too far. We were afraid to be left behind, or run into mine fields.

On the third night my worst fear occurred. A Serbian patrol stopped us in the middle of nowhere on a winding dirt road fully surrounded by trees. Three big men with long beards and hair, armed from head to toe, climbed onto the bus. Bright flashlights stung our eyes as they laughed and told us that we all stank like animals. At that moment, I thought that we would be raped, tortured, or even executed. It was a horrible feeling, and I was so terrified.

Turning their attention to our driver, they asked him if there was "any young entertainment on the bus." Shaking his head, the driver said, "No." The young mother was looking down holding her baby tightly. They kept looking at her and then kept blazing the flashlight in the direction of my sister and me. My sister clearly looked like she was about to die, and I was hiding underneath a big sweater with my hair tangled, trying to look as unattractive as I could, praying for them just to leave us alone. As one of the men was staring at me, his friend called him out saying that they had to go and that there was nothing worth looking at in the pigsty that was our bus. A sense of relief came minutes later when the bus driver turned on the engine and slowly started driving away.

The fourth day I was finally able to get out of the bus for a while and take a real break. I helped elderly people to exit before taking a short break on the bank of a little river. This was an opportunity to get fresh water, wash my face, and stretch my legs.

My sister was so happy to refresh her legs in the cold water. Seeing her smile for the first time in days, I felt for a moment like I was a kid again. This was one of my first moments that I felt movement from fear to greatness on this journey.

That moment passed quickly when a group of military men approached us. I froze, crouching on a rock close to the riverbed, ready to grab my sister and jump if we had to flee. I could not hear what they were saying but later learned that our driver traded cigarettes for information about the best routes to get safely across the Herzegovinian-Croatian border. Those cigarettes likely saved our lives.

Our journey continued and the next morning we arrived in Herzegovina, close to Capljina, a small town where one of my dad's cousins lived. My sister and I decided to take a break before crossing the Croatian border, desperately hoping for a warm shower and food. While we used a phone from the local coffee shop to call our cousin to pick us up, I saw a church in the middle of town.

While my sister rested, I found myself drawn to the little church. As I opened the squeaky door and walked in, it took me a moment to adjust to the darkness. At first I was looking at the walls of the church without understanding what I was seeing. Then it hit me. Holding onto the edge of a pew, the room spun as I saw that the walls were covered with black and white photos of every deceased man and boy from the town, including those that were massacred in their homes.

Each photo had a black ribbon on the upper right corner, a symbol of a deceased person, while their eyes, hundreds and hundreds of their eyes, were staring at me from all directions. I couldn't even find the altar or the statue of Jesus. It must have been taken or destroyed, I thought. Everywhere I turned there were more eyes. Boys who could be no older than 13, and men in their 50s at the most, stared down at me. The ground shook underneath my feet. I felt for a moment that I was in Auschwitz all over again. I felt so nauseous; I was suffocating, fighting for every breath before I managed to reach the door.

As soon as I felt the sunshine on my face and fresh air, I found the strength to walk back to my sister. She was asking me if everything was ok. I managed a weak smile and nod. This was one of the rare occasions where I was at a loss for words.

Reflecting back, this was the moment when I clearly saw the painful evidence of ethnic cleansing, the genocide conducted on Herzegovinian Croats in addition to Bosnian Muslims. Those eyes in those photos in the Church haunted me.

From that moment on, things sped up for us. We lived for a short time in Croatia and Slovenia before beginning our new journey to what I thought was our final destination, Sweden.

I worked with authorities in Zagreb to get our documents in order so that we could get new passports. This was not an easy task since we did not have much documentation to begin with. Rules and policies continually changed, and we even had to prove that we were indeed Croatians!

The more I listened to the news, the more I felt fear and worry for my loved ones left behind. Things were not looking good in many parts of Croatia and Bosnia and Herzegovina. Instinctively, I knew that we would need to get further from the former Yugoslavia not only because my sister needed medical care but also for my protection and safety. I was grateful to my mom's cousin for helping smuggle us through the small border control between Slovenia and Croatia while we were waiting for our documents to get ready.

"Face fear head on so you can achieve your goals and dreams while reaching greatness within you."
~ Izabela, The World Messenger

Many new friends gave us unexpected support during our times of major life transitions. We were showered with human kindness, compassion, and love, even in the moments when they, too, were in difficult situations. I was so grateful to those wonderful people who chose to help us that I started to believe in humanity once again. This was yet another moment when I experienced the movement from fear to greatness on my life journey.

I was also grateful to not be part of the United Nations High Commissioner for Refugee statistics of the estimated 200,000 people killed during the violent breakup of the former Yugoslavia.

Sadly, though, I was part of another statistic as one of the 2.7 million of refugees displaced and dispersed through the world. We were a part of the largest displacement in Europe since the Second World War.

Finding the silver lining in my experience up to this point, I would not have gotten the exposure to the world in such a profound and meaningful way as I did otherwise.

Take Action:

Acknowledging Your Breaking Point

I encourage you to reflect on breaking points you've come across in your life or are currently facing and use these questions to help you determine how you can strive to overcome them and gain the most you can from them.

1. When have you failed? What were contributing factors among your failures?

2. How have you overcome these issues that you have faced?

3. How can you use what you have learned to overcome issues in the future?

Chapter Four

Facing Your Fears

As I have learned numerous times throughout my life, the greatest path toward the truth is experiencing life and its true impact by crawling in its mud in the darkest moments, while eventually being lifted by the wings of its beauty to be celebrated as a whole. It is the same coin; it just depends on what side of the coin you are looking in the moment. It is a dance between heaven and hell, as in Dante's Inferno. It is the never-ending dance between adversity that brings with it the seed of advantage and disadvantage, like Ying and Yang. I finally understood that in every good situation, there is something bad and that in every bad situation, there is something good that can be learned or gained.

As we know, people tend to divide their emotions into "good" or "bad." Fear, highly unpleasant anxiety, gets placed automatically into the "bad" category. What I learned from my personal experiences and from interviewing a wide range of professional athletes and coaches, as well as executive leaders, is that this is not the best way to think about the feeling.

Fear in general wakes you up, makes you more alert to possible threats and makes you more present and aware of your surroundings and things that could go wrong. It makes you think and act in a very different way. It helps you calculate risk very quickly so that you can make fast decisions based on the situation that you are in at a certain moment. It will alert you that something is not right so that you can step back and revisit you choices and decisions.

"First learn how to survive, and then you will be able to thrive on auto pilot." ~ Izabela, The World Messenger

The best part is, if after ticking through that mental list and having everything checked out, it is time to push past that emotional blockage, the fear. The more I reflected on my past experiences, the more fascinating it became. I wanted to know how, what, and why I did things as I did and how different they are now as I am more mature and experienced. Did I act on instinct, following a gut feeling?

I found an undeniable connection between that strong experience of real fear, like when the gun was pointed to my head, and being able to move through the situation with the proper knowledge, expertise, and training. To me, that was the moment when everything else was still. I was fully focused, deeply aware of my surroundings, sounds, people in front of me, his cigarette- and alcohol-saturated breath, his shaking hand, his chilling loud laugh, mixed surprisingly with his own fear behind the façade of a tough guy.

The ability to move through pain, guilt, anger, attack, judgment, defensiveness, and fear in life are the most important factors that will allow you to progress on your path to greatness, to reaching your maximum potential and ultimately your destiny. This ability will continue to develop you in your life constantly, leading you to a new realm of possibilities and the most rewarding opportunities. It is like peeling an onion; more layers will appear, challenging you, yet allowing you to move further than you ever thought was even possible.

How do I know that? I lived through it. I experienced it. And now I am sharing it with you.

Most importantly, it saved my life more than a dozen times and, as a result, many lives of others. My hope is to help you to know the difference if your life ever gets into imminent or perceived danger and kicks your fear into the highest gear.

**"What we can't overcome with fear, we can overcome with love!"
~ Izabela, The World Messenger**

As I was reflecting on overcoming my fears and some of the most complex challenges, including imminent danger that I was exposed to earlier in life, I could not help exploring why and how others deal with that every single day, knowingly putting their lives in danger. I am not talking about the wide range of high-risk jobs like truck drivers, cops, firefighters, construction operators, or fishermen.

I am talking about sports that we love to watch and enjoy seeing at live events, even though we do not fully understand what it takes to play and coach as a pro or true champion and living with the highest ratio of raw fear and risk involved at every second of the game.

Trevor Wittman knows this first hand. He is one of the most recognized and awarded championship coaches and trainers in Mixed Marshal Arts (MMA), kickboxing and boxing.

He has trained over 30 notable MMA fighters such as Georges St-Pierre, Rashad Evans, Shane Carwin, Nate Marquardt, Justin Gaethje, Rose Namajunas and Donald Cerrone, in the Ultimate Fighting Championship (UFC). He has also trained boxers such us Manuel Perez, Verno Philips, Juan Carlos Candelo, and DeAndrey Aborn as well as kickboxers, including Pat Barry and Duane Bang Ludwig.

MMA seems to be the fastest growing sport among fans and MMA to me is the real deal, because it is a true mix of art and style from Boxing, Wrestling, Jiu-Jitsu, Karate, and Kung Fu. If you get a chance to see Trevor's one-of-a-kind training facility called Grudge Training Center near Denver, Colorado, stop by and see where some of the best champions train.

Growing up was not easy for Trevor as a skinny, short, little kid who was told over and over that he was going nowhere and that he was a nobody. Sadly, he grew up believing that in a rough area in Connecticut. At that time in his young life, he did not have much going for himself. He made it to the 10th grade and picked a different path for himself and got into boxing. Becoming a boxer truly changed his life. This was when he began to learn the power of overcoming fear as he stepped into a boxing ring with some scary looking guys.

"Once you understand how powerful your mind is, you really can overcome anything." ~ Trevor Wittman

As he looked across the ring, he would ask himself why he was doing this. Then the bell would ring, and all the fear would be forgotten. After doing this 80 times, Trevor mastered the art of removing fear from his mind and then after a lung injury, he started coaching boxing, then kickboxing, and then migrated to MMA.

As a result, coaching became second nature to him; he has coached all sorts of high- level athletes in championship fights. Trevor even became a star on the reality TV show The Ultimate Fighter. He was a coach on season 10 and season 16.

What Trevor also learned over the years is that if you use your mind correctly, you can accomplish anything you want in this world. The key is to harness that powerful energy into motion and to focus on goals or things you want. Sadly, many people get caught up in thinking about things they don't want, and their energy can lead them down the wrong path without them even knowing.

When you look at Trevor, you see his boyish looks with sparkling blue eyes and feel his playful and joyful energy as he smiles and shares his story. You will also notice how he genuinely probes with questions about you, as he truly wants to learn how he can best assist you and make a positive difference. How refreshing that feels, especially coming from someone who has coached so many true champions in boxing, kickboxing, and MMA.

What he knows so well is that the environment is the key to shedding fear away. After all, what is scarier than fighting another human being inside of a cage? Trevor helps fighters remove fear from their minds as they spar with one another inside a cage on a daily basis. The week before a big main event fight, Trevor holds Media Day at Grudge and allows his fighters to display their talent in front of spectators and cameras.

This particular day is no walk in the park for the fighter because he or she must fight many rounds while facing a new opponent every minute.

After facing that type of adversity in addition to the three-month fight camp itself, Trevor prepares his fighters to remove fear from their vocabulary as they prepare to fight at some of the biggest events that are televised and watched by millions of people around the world.

When you are in the heat of a fight, and you get knocked down, those moments are when fear can take over. But when your mind is right, and you are prepared to overcome adversity, it's easy to get back up and act like nothing happened. In fact, it's fun! That's what Trevor trains his fighters to do and after watching some of these training sessions, I see exactly how he does it.

Trevor is a master at connecting with the soul as he trains his fighters in a one-on- one setting. During these intimate training sessions, he builds their minds up so strong that they don't even know it until adversity hits, and they just bounce back up with a smile and continue to do what they love. Trevor told me that if you are constantly in an environment of severe fear, like a war or gang zone, it is hard to overcome fear on your own, regardless of how positive or optimistic you may be. When you are surrounded with guys who are constantly losing, eventually will start affecting negatively the other guys around them too.

It is essential in Trevor's world to create and preserve an environment of success. You have to create the antidote for fear, which in Trevor's mind is faith. When people are in fear mode, they immediately look at things that will not work with a million explanations of why they would not work, and before you know it you are going very quickly down the rabbit hole to a bottomless stinky pit because they are thinking about what they don't want. Even if a fighter puts himself in that situation, Trevor will force them to find the silver lining.

"When you are ok to have a learning lesson at any given point regardless of the level of your success, then you are moving yourself from being an excellent player to being an exceptional player." ~ Trevor Wittman

After a devastating knockout in UFC 146, Duane "Bang" Ludwig was in the locker room saddened with his head down. He thought he needed to win that fight to buy a dream house for his family. Trevor consoled Duane and said, "This was supposed to happen. Good things are coming your way." Two years later, Duane retired from the UFC to become a coach for Team Alpha Male, and he won coach of the year in 2013 and 2014. Needless to say, he got his dream house.

Trevor also believes that facing and overcoming fear is a good thing that helps you to be a better and stronger person capable of going further than you ever allowed yourself to go. It is a matter of perspective. If you are ok to put yourself in the boxing ring and are willing to lose the fight and still believe that you can win the championship, then you are on the right path. What I found to be very uplifting through my conversation with Trevor was his interpretation of failure. As long as you know you gave something your best, and you are working as hard as possible to better yourself, then you did not fail; you are learning and progressing. This simple yet profound mindset will propel you forward. It is just that simple.

For example, if it is a rainy day, then instead of being gloomy and listing the things it may ruin, focus on the positive: it will water your plants, make your lawn greener, and cool off the hot summer day. But what we can learn here is that every situation has its own visible and, often, hidden benefits.

"When you stand naked in the truth there is nothing to fear!" ~ Izabela, The World Messenger

At the end of the day, choose your environment and the people around you carefully, as they can make you or break you. Think for a second about TV and the media. If you watch reality programming, you will expose yourself to an earthshaking fear factor that can be paralyzing and defeating before you even gave yourself a chance to be or do something. As a result, too many people will never challenge themselves and will always opt for easy solutions and quick, temporary rewards. So many people will never explore what they are truly capable of.

Sadly, many people will turn into haters instead of successful people, fabricating reasons why someone else is succeeding more than they are. I am sure you have heard versions of these conversations too many times already. But if you embrace the challenges, learn from the difficulties, and take it one step at a time, you can make a positive shift in your life and your environment and you will start to witness magic unfolding.

And yes my dear friend, you are worth it! Do not let anyone under the sun or moon and stars tell you otherwise. You have my permission to be bold and to be the best version of you.

"I am here to cheer you up, pick you up, push you, and most of all shower you with unconditional love in the process!"
~ Izabela, The World Messenger

Trevor has witnessed many things rapidly unfold as a result of chain reactions around people in negative as well as positive environments. To know at any given moment where you are and what is going on with you, it is so important to harness self-awareness. Many people see what is going on in someone's life, but they can't see what is going in their own life. As a result, we miss knowing what is going on in our state of mind.

Does anything positive happen when you are in a negative state of mind? Not from my experience! In the very instant when we have negative thinking, communicating, decision-making, and overall living, we have a negative relationship with the people around us and within ourselves.

Many of you may say, "But Izabela, all this is a matter of perception." Bingo! It is! You are spot on. Perception is also another very big component to understanding what, why, and how we fear. Fear is purely a state of mind, and you are in control of it (or not). Only our mind can produce fear, nothing else!

Likewise, only our mind can produce positive thought. The fact is our whole life is one big experiment!

Personally, after the horrors of the war despite letting go of the past, I can't watch bloody fights as I did with my dad when I was five or six years old. I appreciate the spirit of the fighter, and know that they are doing this professionally by their own personal choice and within the rules and regulations. But what I respect the most is that they are not using and abusing their unique talents and skills to break or beat others outside of sports, not playing "the tough guys" with regular people, especially children and women. Kudos to those champions who do know the difference and are serving as role models to youth! Sadly, so many kids are often bullied, picked on, and are struggling with their self-worth due to a wide range of environments that they are exposed to on a daily base in their school and at home.

As I was working on this book, my friend, Preston Rahn was working on a book too. So one Saturday night, an unusual way to spend a weekend evening for some, we would interject to ask each other questions and then carry on with our tasks.

Preston that night opted to take a break from writing and watch the UFC Championship event in Mexico City through his online account. There were five or six fights, finishing up with a final championship.

I would quickly look at each opponent and tell him before they would even start the fight who was going to win. He said, "Yeah, right Izabela." I smiled and continued with my work. The first time my guy won, he would ask me who would win next by showing me quickly both fighters standing next to each other. I would quickly take a look and tell him who would be the winner. I did that five times that evening and every single time I "guessed" according to him 100%. He was puzzled. He asked me, "How did you know that without even knowing who these guys are?" I smiled.

Quickly I replied, "100% based on my instincts and intuition." I would look at each player, and I would "scan them" to see who was emotionally ready to win or who was in a state of fear. It is all in how you carry yourself, how you look at the other opponent in the eyes, where your energy is coming from, and what you believe at the moment before the fight. It is that simple.

At that moment, I could not help but remember my dad and our special times together watching sports and discussing who would win and who would lose. I smiled peacefully, knowing that my life experiences contributed yet again to that deep profound knowledge. I would know in a second who is coming from fear and being within the fear, and who is coming to the game as a warrior or gladiator, ready to put on the best fight that they can.

Ironically a few weeks later I would learn the night I was working with Preston, Trevor Wittman, from the Grudge Training Center, was there to support his championship candidate. Apparently, his candidate got sick in the middle of a fight. Mexico City has an elevation of almost 7,300 ft., and Trevor's fighter Nate had trouble breathing and began taking a pummeling without being able to defend himself very well.

Trevor jumped on the cage and tried stopping the fight, but the UFC has a rule that only a doctor or the referee can stop the fight. When the bell rang for that round to end, Trevor immediately waived his arms as he entered inside the octagon (fighting space) to support his fighter. The referee did grant the stoppage request, and now the UFC is considering adopting "The Wittman Rule" which would allow coaches to stop the fight if their candidate is getting hurt too badly.

Some games get us connected to people, teams, fans, and families that we know personally and professionally. Some events leave us wondering why and what we could have changed or improved. And some simply leave us puzzled, searching for the answer, sometimes over the course of our lifetime...

Take Action:

Facing Your Fears

Whether you dread that spider on your ceiling or are anxious about your future, we all fear something. By clearly identifying your fear(s) (with the help of these questions), you are one step closer to overcoming it.

1. What are the fear(s) you face?

2. Have you taken any steps to overcoming your fear(s)?

3. Have you been successful in overcoming your fears? What are you hoping to gain as a result of overcoming them?

Chapter Five

Defeating Your Demons

My sister's and my journey continued the path to freedom. In hindsight, I realized that I had to go through a major breaking point in my young adult life while discovering my true life purpose, my big WHY, by defeating my demons.

Our plan was to seek political asylum in Sweden and reconnect with our brother, Igor. Unfortunately, we couldn't just jump on a plane or take a train through Austria and Germany due to politics and border regulations. In the end, we had only one option. Our trip had to be by bus through Eastern Europe, yet another long journey with a lot of risks.

As I was assuring my sister that this would be a quick and very rewarding trip for us during our last night in Zagreb, I walked to the bus station to buy two one-way tickets to Sweden. At that moment, I felt that in many ways that this was the point of no return.

I was going to seek political asylum without fully understanding all of its implications, seeking one country, one nation to open their doors to two young women from what used to be Yugoslavia. I kept hoping that Sweden would accept us, allow us to stay and offer us the opportunity to have refuge in their country.

"We can overcome the darkest and most uncertain moments in life through seeking refuge within by embracing change with open arms and an open heart." ~ **Izabela, The World Messenger**

That night I slept very little, as I played a million scenarios in my mind while checking on our bags time and time again to be certain that we had our most important possession, a one month supply of insulin for my sister. I kept visualizing the outcome I was seeking while forcing my racing brain to slow down so I could get some sleep. I tried to pray a little in my own way, which was hard for me to do since I was so conflicted with so many emotions.

This new journey was nerve-wracking in its own way since we had to go through so many borders and patrols. I just kept thinking and seeing in my mind the map of Europe with a bright blue star pinned to our final destination, Malmo, Sweden. Our brother was already somewhere in Sweden at that time, and we could not wait to find him. I longed to hug him and tell him all that had happened back home. I desperately needed to talk to someone who would understand. After all, he was the older brother who would always pay attention to what was happening in my world, just in case I needed his protection.

Some things will never change regardless of how old we may be. I remember when we were in kindergarten. At one point, the three of us siblings were nearby each other in different groups based on our ages. During lunchtime, we often had special activities, where all the groups were combined, watching a show or TV.

At those special occasions, I was happy to run into my brother and sit close to him. Since I was small and shy, I felt protected knowing that he could look after me if someone would give me a hard time. Boys would push me around until I learned to tell them no or tell them to push my brother next time. It was funny how quickly they would run in the opposite direction and leave me alone.

Between us siblings, we had an unspoken rule "One for all, and all for one" that we discovered its deeper meaning through one of our all-time favorite movies, "The Three Musketeers."

Once, a slightly older girl from my sister's group was hysterical and started scratching my face with her sharp nails, leaving a small scar I still have to this day on my face. My brother came running, pulling me back as I was standing crying without understanding what and why this was happening. This was a bittersweet lesson I learned that sometimes people do very mean things with no clear or obvious reason. Also, I learned to value and cherish my siblings, being keenly aware that my life would not be the same if I had been an only child.

In my mind, it was understandable that with a deep love for my sister and concern for her wellbeing I would face another challenge to bring her to safety and urgently needed healthcare. Our new journey started with crossing the border with Hungary, then what was still Czechoslovakia, and then Poland. As we passed the first passport patrol, I was on pins and needles until we got through the second border with Czechoslovakia. The bus driver gave us instructions on what to say and to stay calm regardless of what may happen.

As we were going through the last part of Hungary, in the middle of nowhere, on the side roads right before the border, we started seeing many trucks parked on the dusty side roads and women in high heels and little clothing standing around, looking emotionally detached, apathetic, and waiting for men to approach them.

I felt like someone kicked me in the stomach because we were in the middle of nowhere, and I saw all this open prostitution with many young girls. I was outraged, scared and shocked all at the same time because I didn't like what I saw, and I didn't want that to happen to me. I prayed that we would be able to get to the other side of the border safely. Luckily my sister was napping and missed seeing all of this.

The bus driver took our passports to the border patrol guards. Finally came back with a smile on his face. He told us that we were cleared and ready to go through. I looked at him with disbelief but as we approached the patrol station, two guards waived for us to pass through. As we were crossing through, I noticed two young girls providing adult entertainment for the guards. I was in complete disbelief. I guess that's why they were in such a good mood and let us go through so easily. When I got my passport back, I held it in my hand so tightly that my hand hurt for days afterword. I wanted so much to cry, but I had not been able to release even a single teardrop since the war began. I began to wonder if I would ever be able to cry again, if I would ever be able to release all of the sorrows buried deep inside of me.

The further we got, the more relieved I felt. Finally, we were at the Polish border. As I was sitting next to my sister on the bus, a young Polish man came in with a flashlight to check our documents. He was looking at each photo and person twice, making sure that they matched.

In English, he asked me, "Where are you going?" Without even thinking I replied, "Sweden." He looked at me and asked, "Why Sweden?" With a smile, I told him that we were on our way to visit our brother. On the way back to the front of the bus, he took all of our travel documents and asked us to wait. It was another nerve-wracking moment. Even though our papers were in order, I was still not sure if they would let us go through Poland and on to Sweden.

The minutes passed by as if they were hours. I thought about our last holiday celebration as a whole family, in peace, surrounded by family and friends, laughter, love, and humor. I held onto that mental picture without realizing what I was doing: I was recreating an positive emotional charge by trying to access the positive feelings that I held inside me.

The border patrol officer came back and handed our passports to the driver. Then the driver called my name. I was startled. He asked me if I could help him to return passports to everyone in the bus. I guess it made sense since we were sitting up front, the second row behind him.

I was so relieved knowing that if everything went as planned, we would be in Sweden the next morning. In a sense, I began to think of my passport as my Olympic torch. Each hurdle passed was a victory on this long journey to freedom.

"To move forward in life you have to face your inner demons!"
~ Izabela, The World Messenger

The next morning, as we approached the sun-covered buildings looking for the ferry, my first impression of Sweden was promising: homes were colorful, clean, and welcoming. I finally breathed a sigh of relief on our fourth day of this journey. The driver wished all of us good luck as we got out of the bus and headed to the control station.

Everything about the next bit of time is foggy and difficult to remember. We were bombarded with a million questions through interpreters with accents very hard to understand. We were required to go through a full body search, and we had to provide all of our documents that were then collected, copied, and added to our file. This is how our asylum seeking process began.

I felt stripped down to the core, naked, vulnerable, desperately wanting to know what might happen next. I had a million questions and very few answers. But at that moment I had a new determination – to find the right answers on my own from the Swedish authorities.

By the time each of us separately finished our statement for political asylum, I was happy to be finally reunited with my sister and to see how she was doing. Seeing her smiling face and giving her a hug never felt as good as it did at that moment. I looked at her and promised that from now on things would be a piece of cake without knowing how, but deep down feeling determined that it simply would.

We were given a key to our room in a transitional "hotel," which looked more or less like a hostel or juvenile correctional facility with security guards and people from all over the world. I guess this was not what I had envisioned as I daydreamed of traveling as a young girl with a deep desire to explore the world. It was intense, way too intense for me who had just come from a torn country and survived the hellish journey to Sweden. So many different languages were spoken.

People were behaving in many different ways than I was used to. Some people were arguing, even fighting with each other, and this put me back on a "high alert" that lasted until we finally moved to a small town after months at the transitional "hotel" and started rebuilding our lives. This was the major new starting point and a release for my sister and me. As we were unloading this magnitude of stress, emotional pain, and profound sadness, we started to feel better, yet I still could not cry. I would not understand why I could not shed any tears until several years later.

Right before our move, I encountered a young man from Rwanda who transformed my vision of who I am and what I was all about once again. He happened to be in Holland and Denmark when the genocide of Tutsis took place in April of 1994. After the genocide had occurred, he was visiting his friends in Sweden when we "accidentally" briefly met. He was a handsome, tall, young African man standing in front of me, looking like he just stepped out of a Rolling Stone magazine shoot – a hip yet classy artist with dark eyes looking at me with a mixture of pain, sadness, anger, and something that may have once resembled love. He asked me where I was from in English, and I shyly replied Yugoslavia. He looked me straight in the eyes and said, "They choose to help you but not us." These words immediately cut me deeply and shredded me to pieces.

With tears in my eyes while I was biting my lower lip, I tried hard just to listen. It was hard, very hard. Everything in me was screaming, "No, no this is not true!" until I realized that this was the other side of the coin with his truth on it, painful, raw, and real. I looked at him with tears in my eyes that I was holding and fighting back once again and softly whispered, "I am sorry" while bowing my head down as I stood there in front of him feeling once again helpless and paralyzed.

"Look in your heart to heal deep sorrows while letting your tears lead you to most profound truths."
~ Izabela, The World Messenger

His truth was real, so real! 800,000 men, woman, and children perished in the Rwandan genocide, 800,000 red rose buds and petals thrown in the mud and lost forever. Lost lives and their beauty for what? I felt horrible that parts of history were repeating, where attackers came from within the country, disguised as fellow neighbors like in Yugoslavia. I was choking, like an inside of me there was a deep ocean of endless sadness.

I already deeply struggled with my own "survivor's guilt" from the Balkan war. Now his words of "They choose to help them, but not us" echoed in my mind, chilling me to the core. As I raised my head, our eyes met and for a moment we kept looking at each other, me just staring until I snapped out of my trance and truly looked at him with deep understanding and acceptance. And then something magical happened. I ran and gave him a hug saying, "I am so sorry!"

He hugged me back holding me so tight, sobbing. He cried holding onto me without letting go and then I witnessed the most beautiful smile with glistening white diamonds and full lips. He kissed my forehead and gently removed my tangled hair. His gestures were so real, loving, and respectful. My soft hair was reflecting something new and unknown, something that just fascinated him in addition to a deep longing for his loved ones and an uncertainty about their whereabouts back home.

Then I recognized the survivor's guilt in him too. He was on his way to Amsterdam to the opening of his art show after his trip to the UK when all hell broke loose in Rwanda. I could not, for the life of me at that time, understand the politics and choices that helped one group of people but not others. In my mind, human life was the most precious gift regardless of race, skin color, gender, or political or economic position.

"If we held 1 minute of silence for every victim of the Holocaust then we would be silent for 11 1/2 years" ~ **Unknown**

When I read this the first time, the sorrow and sadness that I felt at that moment was so profound that I thought for a moment that I will drown. When this fact sank in my head, I started thinking how many minutes of silence it would take for all the lost lives of my fellow Yugoslavian citizens and Rwandans. That imagined silence got longer and longer as I encountered more refugees from Somalia, Ethiopia, and other places.

In that brief exchange between us, so much was understood yet left unspoken. His friends came, and he had to go. I stood in the same place frozen, wondering, did this just happen? Did I imagine this?

As the years pass by I often go to that moment of deep human connection, mutual understanding, and deep profound presence – the type of moment when we discover the depth of our hearts, profound universal truths, and open our minds beyond our imaginations. To me, this was a glimpse of the unconditional love that I knew so well in what seems like lifetimes ago and somehow let go of in the process of going to hell and back. And in that very moment, I wanted to hold on to nothing but the love in my heart.

This was my first touch, hug, and kiss on my cheek by a young African man. I could not stop from thinking for a moment about the photographs that I used to get from orphanages in Africa from Mother Theresa's charity, making me feel more connected than ever with the world.

I learned to find comfort in my daily walks and morning runs and limited Swedish TV programming. At the same time, I was fully immersed in learning the Swedish language. I was getting ready for a long interview with our lawyer, and I did not want to leave anything out that might help my sister and me. I refused to depend on assistance from other people as I witnessed the poor quality of interpretation and translation for my sister firsthand during her first doctor visit.

In my mind, the stakes were too high to leave this in someone else's hands. In a million years, I never imagined that I could learn Swedish so quickly. Within four months, I had reached an intermediate level that would allow me to assist thousands of refugees from what was now the former Yugoslavia, in addition to my sister and me.

"Master something worth mastering, something that will generate significant value to the world. You will automatically increase your value exponentially!"
~ Izabela, The World Messenger

A month later as I was sitting on the dock and listening to the light waves reaching the shore, I decided that I was going to be happy. I was going to skip even if I was walking on muddy paths; I would sing regardless of whether the birds were the only ones who could hear me. I was going to smile again, more often, and often with no thoughts of what others may think.

I was going to celebrate life every day and its small wonderful special moments. I would be open and loving. I was going to count my blessings and look for positive things I would have. I was going to daydream and dream again. I was going to be truly happy. But to achieve that, I needed to find inner peace – the first stepping stone on my path to happiness.

Honestly, I never expected that it would take such a long time to be able to arrive at that state effortlessly and consistently, regardless of what the current situation may be. But I am glad that it did start back then with that first baby step that helped me to arrive at my desired destination at the perfect time.

Due to my linguistic and cross-cultural knowledge, I was often interviewed in local Swedish newspapers, TV, and radio. This was especially the case around the time of the Dayton Agreement. I became a voice for the voiceless since they weren't able to or feared to share their stories. I prayed to God to never again have another conversation like the one I did with the young man from Rwanda.

After multiple interviews on one particular day with national radio stations and newspapers, I came home emotionally drained to find my sister waiting for me. Instantly, I sensed that something was wrong. I could tell that her sweet, soft spoken demeanor could not hide that she was preparing to tell me something awful, something that would crush my world all over again.

That same day, the day before the agreement was officially signed in Dayton and the fighting would stop in Bosnia and Herzegovina, I lost my childhood hero – my uncle. He was one of several instrumental role models in my life who would do anything for me. He taught me how to ride a horse. He was the one that taught me how to drive a stick shift when I was only 14. He was the one who introduced me to MMA and boxing for fun and self-defense.

He was my rock at my dad's funeral, risking his life to be there by my side, cheering me up, and putting a smile on my face. He was the one who came to say goodbye to my sister and me as we were fleeing and gave me money to carry with us on our journey to freedom. He was the one who could have had a first class lifestyle in Switzerland with permanent residency, but he refused to leave our native country. He wanted to be there, on the ground, to protect us when no one else would.

This was one of the hardest losses for me to swallow because he meant so much to me. For the first time, I couldn't hold in my outrage. When my sister told me what happened, I hit the wall so hard with my fists that I was in pain for days, but I did not care because the pain inside me was a million times worse. I yelled "Why, why now? Why him? Why? Why?" while I continued hitting the wall as hard as I could.

That night I ran for hours, to the point that I could not move any longer. I was shivering and shaking. As I sat on the ground, I looked up at the dark sky with the glistening stars and seconds later a comet streaked across the sky. And at that moment I asked, "Why God? Why him? Why now? It's the end of the war, the very end!

How could you God?" When I didn't get an answer, I felt completely defeated. When I finally found the strength to talk to my family in Croatia weeks later, I learned that my uncle's team was on a special mission protecting another city when one of his teammates fell from a cliff. Without hesitation, he volunteered to go down and pick up his friend's body.

His words right before his last mission were ***"No mother in this world deserves to not bury her own fallen son – I have to do this."*** He did not have any difficulty getting to the bottom of the canyon since he was extremely fit and athletic. The problem was that he ran into a minefield set up by Serbian troops. He stepped on one with his left heel, and he bled to death.

As he was lying down, dying he had a voice recorder that recorded his last message to his family, his son, and his wife, who was pregnant at that time. Even to this day, I cannot listen to his last words as he was dying, telling how cold he was, and how thirsty even though he was just inches away from the river. People like him are impossible to replace, leaving deep voids that not even the most amazing childhood memories can fill.

As I was waiting to hear the status of my political asylum application in Sweden, I worked in refugee camps as a professional interpreter and translator (yes, in Swedish) and as an educator in kindergarten with preschool kids, which I enjoyed very much. After a year and a half of working with the same group of kids, one day during recess, I started to feel little pebbles hitting my skin. I looked at the direction where they were coming from and saw a bunch of kids from my group throwing the pebbles at me.

I said, "Please stop, it hurts." They started laughing and started yelling "blackhead, blackhead" at me, which was a bad racial remark for someone from another race, essentially saying that I was less valuable or important. I was shocked and speechless. Is this really happening? As I turned my head in the direction of the kindergarteners, a 53 year-old man, Magnus, the head of the facility was just standing and watching without doing or saying anything. He was silent, completely ignoring what was happening. I was speechless.

I walked into the building and picked up my stuff and ran away as far and as fast as I could without ever returning. I was heartbroken. My work with these kids was never an issue until that moment. I loved those kids. I felt that we bonded well in that year and a half and that we had worked together well. I was so shocked at what had just happened. I was not mad at them but at Magnus who, despite being an educator, was a complacent witness, looking at me coldly and dismissing me like I was a parasite.

I was shocked that this happened even as I worked so hard to help others rebuild their lives within the Swedish society. As I was actively working in the community, supporting Swedish officials with refugee resettlement, and providing my linguistic services, I also played tennis, hockey, and field hockey with some of the Swedish youth. I started dance and music programs with my friends to help integrate Swedish youth with refugees from all over the world. After the initial shock of the pebble incident had worn off, I began to realize that the situation had nothing to do with me. It just gave me another reason to be even more fearless.

"Don't let hate poison your mind, body, heart or soul! Before you know it, you will lose peace within yourself, love and all!"
~ Izabela, The World Messenger

That incident inspired me to take action and explore other options. Through months of hard work and numerous applications to Canada, the UK, New Zealand, and Australia, I finally found a little doorway to my childhood dream – the US. I was lucky to find out that my aunt, a physics professor, and my uncle, formerly an agent with the Yugoslavian equivalent to the FBI agent, ended up in the US and I wanted so badly to go there too.

I was tired of living in so many different places, continually re-establishing myself over and over, starting and stopping my education, learning new languages, and adapting to new cultures without any guarantee that I could even stay there. I was seeking something permanent, solid, and somewhere I could build my new life as an independent young woman.

Through my newly established connections, family support, and personal determination, I found an opportunity for which I was willing to risk everything I had. The next day I did something that changed the course of my life forever. Without a father, mentor, or anyone else to consult with, I dressed professionally and walked in without an appointment to the town hall building. I told the clerk that I wanted to see the mayor. He looked at me puzzled and asked if I had an appointment. I looked at him straight in the eyes and said, "This is an extremely urgent matter that requires his immediate attention." He was blushing, puzzled, and clumsy. He ran to the mayor's office and two minutes later walked back with the mayor.

The mayor looked at me as I repeated, "Please, this is an extremely urgent matter, and it will take only five minutes of your time." My posture exuded nothing but seriousness and urgency. He shook my hand as I introduced myself, and he walked me to his office.

"Only human spirit can show us what is possible by taking far reaching goals and risks along the journey of life!"
~ Izabela, The World Messenger

I was offered a seat, and I responded by telling him the following in perfect Swedish, "Let's not waste anyone's time here. I am a political asylum seeker from the former Yugoslavia and have been waiting for my application to be reviewed for the past three years. I am tired of waiting. I am here to ask you to grant me a six months visa. I need to go to Vienna to interview with the American consul and prove my refugee status so that I can go to the US. If I get denied, I can't go back home. I will be killed.

I need to be able to come back and hope for the best. If I leave Sweden without a visa, my political asylum application will be immediately terminated. This way we may have a win-win for both of us. For you – one less refugee to worry about; for me permanent residency where I can rebuild my life." And then, I handed him my passport. He looked at me surprised and speechless. I just stood in front of him and kept looking straight in his eyes. He got up slowly and told me that he would be back shortly. He came back with a six-month visa in my passport!

Less than five minutes later, I was outside of the building facing below 22 degrees Celsius (- 8 Fahrenheit) of chilling cold. Yet I never felt so warm in my heart and soul. This was one of my sweetest victories yet on my journey to freedom. This moment was an opening to the future that I was intentionally creating, intentionally not letting things just happen to me. I claimed my power back and I felt like the richest person in the world.

I walked into the apartment that my sister and I lived in. I walked in with a heavy heart. I had to tell her and my brother that it was time for me to chase my own dreams and leave Sweden, which also meant I'd be leaving them behind.

My sister was in a very good place; healthy and active, with full access to healthcare and the diet she needed to have a healthy lifestyle. She decided to go to nursing school while my brother was blazing through his MBA program. Life was very good and very promising for both of them. And at that moment, I felt that I had fulfilled my promise to my dad. It felt so good, beyond words.

"Do not reject what you don't understand at the moment; deep understanding may bring acceptance; acceptance may bring the most profound love!" **~ Izabela, The World Messenger**

That was how I started to create my own opportunities, claiming back my inner power that I define as my own Super Power. I felt invincible during my interaction with the mayor, and I could not wait to continue repeating that feeling. I once again had a strong faith within me that when I got to Vienna I would be able to prove my refugee status and get permanent residency in the US. My childhood dream just may come true after all. This was a new challenge I was ready to take on, as I had already faced and defeated so many internal and external demons. But this time I was 100% on my own.

Take Action:

Defeating Your Demons

Do you know what your demons are? If not, you are not alone, these questions will help you identify them and distinguish the best ways to defeat them.

1. What demons haunt you and make it hard to sleep at night?

2. What actions can you take to defeat your demons?

3. How were you successful in defeating your demons?

Chapter Six

Identifying Your WHY

My new journey, after leaving Sweden started first in Frankfurt, Germany and continued to Austria. By the time I arrived in Vienna, I was ready for my meeting with the American ambassador. As I waited for my turn, I observed a wide range of people waiting with fear and anxiety about what the outcome would be that day. For me just being here was a victory. When my name was called, I felt like I was on Cloud Nine.

I walked in and firmly shook the ambassador's hand and looked at him straight in the eye. He was stern and asked me to take a seat. A professional interpreter was in the room, and she began to explain the process to me. I looked at her, smiled and told her that I didn't need an interpreter. The ambassador raised his eyebrows and said that we should have her in the room, "just in case." I agreed.

"You are magically unstoppable when your soul is lit on fire!"
~Izabela, The World Messenger

He started by asking me some simple questions and I replied back in my broken British English. I kept going without worrying if I sounded funny or about my occasional poor use of grammar. Ten to fifteen minutes into our conversation, he stood up, shook my hand and said, "Welcome to America – you are approved. Make it your American dream! You will do so well – you took the initiative to speak on your own. We need more people like you! Now we just need to decide where you should go. Your choices are New York City, Los Angeles or Phoenix. Where would you like to go?" I replied immediately, "Denver, Colorado."

He looked at me a bit confused and said that Denver's not on the list. I looked him straight in the eyes, without thinking, bold, fearless, and daring, as I replied, "But it is on mine." He chuckled, shook his head and said "Ok, Denver it is. Make arrangements with my assistant and all the best to you." At that moment I could hear one of John Denver's songs in my head, and I could not wait to see the blue sky over the Rocky Mountains in Colorado.

At that moment, the only thing I could think of was "... take me home, take me home..." from the song. I was so ready to build my new life in my new home.

I smiled as I thanked him on my way out. Then I realized I had a double victory!

I was going to Denver, the city of my choice. That meant that I had to reside in Denver for the first year of my immigration to the U.S. and check in on a monthly basis with a refugee resettlement agency that sponsored my first 90 days in the country. I was not ready to live in a large city like Los Angeles or New York, nor was I ready to live in Phoenix, a desert. Besides, I was hoping to connect with my aunt and uncle, who lived in Denver and were the only family that I had on American soil.

Second, I finally got permanent residency in the US, making my childhood dream come true. On my way out to the metro, I was skipping and smiling full of joy. I was a six year old again wishing to share so badly my news with my dad, but I knew that he was with me every step of the way on this journey and knew about all of my victories.

"Let your heart show the way, lead the way and find the way – NOW!" ~ Izabela, The World Messenger

It took another six to eight months before I finally got on a plane to America. Getting my immunization and immigration paperwork in order was a piece of cake this time around. My trip to the US was long, with multiple connections and delays due to winter storms on the East Coast, but a lot nicer than the bus trips I took when I had fled my homeland.

When I landed in the US, I took a deep breath and thanked God and the Universe. I was so grateful. Without knowing it at that moment, the most important part of my life's journey was just beginning.

My first impression of Denver, Colorado was magnificent. I met new friends and enjoyed the people, the friendliness, the sunshine and endless opportunities. As I settled in, I had more and more conversations about how I got here. When I spoke to people in a wide range of settings, a common thread was that they kept asking me, "How did you survive all the crazy things you had to face as a young adult?" The conversation typically followed with me explaining how I found what I come to call my "WHY."

This led me to start thinking and reflecting on my past experiences. I realized that early on I had to learn how to be emotionally independent and resilient. As a result, I learned early on how much it matters how we respond or react to what we experience in life.

"You are your life creator: with or without your limiting beliefs."
~ Izabela, The World Messenger

Another lesson that I learned early in my life was that when we depend on others to build us up, rather than to depend on ourselves, we also give them the power to break us down. I knew that if I allowed myself to break down, I would not have survived the war.

I did not want to lose my life in vain. It needed to be worth something more than egocentric, idiotic, and brain-washed ideologies of pure power and control. I learned that I do not need validation from others to know my self-worth. I learned how to rise above and move forward in life.

Why? I am here on a mission, I am here with a big vision, and I am here to fulfill big dreams. Truth be told, I am here to leave a legacy. Not just mine, but also my dad's, my mom's, my grandma's, and all those who prematurely departed but left their dreams and desires unfulfilled due to their selflessness and self-sacrifice in order to save and positively impact others.

When we depend on others to validate our sense of self, then we truly do not know who we are and that is reflected in our personal and romantic relationships, at work and among our colleagues, as well as with our coaches and teammates.

By accepting ourselves and modifying our thinking until we reach the best version of ourselves, and take active strides to be true and authentic toward who we are, how we feel, and behave, I believe that we can obtain at some point that magical inner sense of peace and independence that we work towards. To reach that, you need to have a goal or dream bigger than yourself, bigger than your life. That is how you discover your WHY! When you have that, you can dare to move forward even if you don't yet know your next step.

Further, it is critical to know the WHY that motivates you and drives you to push yourself further than you would have yesterday. Both successful professional athletes and business leaders are clear on their why, and they are committed to reaching their goals regardless of obstacles that they encounter along the way. The fact that things are not going our way in a specific moment does not mean that we are not making progress or that we can't succeed in the end.

Let me share with you the personal story of a very private, humble, yet powerful and tremendously successful man who I admire, Mike Haynes. Mike Haynes is a former National Football League (NFL) cornerback and a Hall of Fame athlete. I felt very lucky to be introduced to him through my great mentor and friend, Jim Roncevich.

Mike had a very successful career in professional American Football (he played for the New England Patriots and Los Angeles Raiders) during an era where not many players got to play professionally for 15 years. He was lucky, or better yet he was very smart. He stayed on top of his game – keeping himself lean, fit, and fast.

Mike was known as the "Gentlemen Raider" during a time full of many scandals in the personal and professional lives of players.

But this is not the main reason I felt lucky to have met him. Mike is a great human being, man, father, husband, role model, leader, and influencer. He is also a successful speaker, prostate cancer survivor, advocate, businessman, coach, mentor, and one of the key influencers and advocates in the NFL who is making positive changes within the League regarding regulations for players in conjunction with coaches and team owners.

As a kid from Europe, I didn't know about American football rules until I met and learned more through Mike, as well as other former players like Keith Lee and Merrill Hodge. Since being taught the intricacies, I can now truly appreciate the game.

As an early beginning, when you are a kid, you simply don't know what you don't know. I am sure that all of us can relate to that. For instance, in baseball, maybe you're not a great hitter, so no one sees you as a great baseball player, and maybe not even a great athlete. This can quickly shatter your dreams. This almost happened to Mike, but he realized that baseball was just not his sport, and so he went on to try football. Unless you try multiple sports, you never know where your true talent might be.

"As a kid, you simply don't know what you don't know."
~ Mike Haynes

Finding the right sport to play as a kid is so important. I am sure it kept so many of us up late at night hoping to make a team. You can't just show up and say, "My dad was a great football player, so I'm going to be a great football player too." You may have your dad's talents or you may not. Maybe you're going to be a good wrestler. The key is to help kids find that sport that they both excel in and also enjoy.

You may already know how Mike's story ends as a professional Hall of Fame athlete, but you may not know how he started.

Mike grew up in Los Angeles as an inner-city kid and life was not easy for him and his family. His mom wouldn't let him play youth football, so instead he played little league baseball, some basketball, and he also ran track. Mike only started playing football when he was in the 10th grade. He didn't know if he could tackle or even had any football talent at all. But he gave football a try and soon realized that he was just as good as the other guys on the team. In fact, he started to excel in catching and throwing and was fast, very fast. Running track and staying fit had paid off for Mike.

When Mike was playing football, he wasn't out there to show everyone he was way faster, or much better; he was just out there doing whatever the coach asked him to do. At that time, he never felt like he was a great athlete. But Mike had a very big WHY!

He wanted to go to college, and he saw a new opportunity that could change his life – an athletic scholarship while playing the sport he started to truly love. He wanted to change the environment that he was a part of as an inner-city teen, as well to work on himself to be the best he can be.

At first, he was not selected to play in the high school all-star game. He knew that his only chance to accomplish his goal was to play in the front of the scouts at that game. Initially, he wanted to be a wide receiver but when his coach asked him, "which one, fourth or fifth? He answered, "What else I can do well so I can play at the all-star game?" He knew he didn't have a chance to play as a wide receiver.

He found a magic solution. During the all-star game, Mike asked the coach if he could play in a different position, as a defensive back because he figured that he could beat a certain player. His coach agreed to the position switch.

The same position that he beat that guy out at is the same position that he is in the hall of fame for in both collegiate and professional football. Ironically, Mike hadn't played in the position before that game, but he felt in his gut that he could still play better than the other guy even though he had no coaching in that position. He followed his intuition, but he had also studied the game, so he knew enough about what the position entailed.

At that time, he still didn't know how to tackle properly, but he wasn't afraid of tackling. Mike just would not give up. He was relentless. In college, he learned to work on his form and perfect his technique by playing as a defensive back.

Mike discovered how his talent fit within a team. A team is made up of a lot of people playing a lot of different positions, and a lot of different personalities. Sometimes you can have a couple of guys who aren't on the same page as everybody else. As a football player, Mike learned that when the roles and goals were not clear, people failed to function as a team.

For example, if you take the business analogy of a CEO who has a goal for the company to do a billion dollars in sales, but he doesn't communicate that goal at all to the employees, then there is no way for the company to all pull in the same direction towards that goal. Only the CEO knows the goal. Key players might unknowingly be working against that goal. Instead, if the CEO of the company says, "Let's get together and let's create a plan that's going to get us to a billion dollars," then everyone at that point is working together, or at least shares the same vision on how to achieve the goal.

On NFL teams, everybody wants to go to the Super Bowl. So what do we need to do to get to the Super Bowl? For Mike as he got older, he got smarter. He realized that all he needed to do was perform his job the best that he could. He felt that to go to the Super Bowl, he needed to make sure that everyone he came in contact with was helping him do his job, and that he was helping them do their job, because by helping them do their job he was essentially helping them do his job as well. In the end, everyone who contributes, increases the chance of winning exponentially. That is how you can win your championship!

As a player, when people would often say, "Mike, you're the greatest defensive back, you're so awesome," he could just say thank you and walk away, but he didn't. He would stop and say, "I couldn't do it without the help of my team." He would mention the guys, his defensive line, and his defensive coordinator. He would give recognition where he thought it was due.

It is important to share successes with your team whether in sports or business, even if you are a one man show, CEO, golf player, or tennis player. People will go out of their way to support you even more when you act like a true leader and team player. It is just that simple. Respect others, and the contributions of others, then others will respect you.

Besides having respect, you need to have a plan. Mike and his team had a plan. Every single week they would review their successes as well as the opportunities for improvement. Here's a look into Mike's team performance review: *"That guy didn't do his job, but he's got a sore leg, we have an excuse for it. So, we need to get him healthy. Who's working to get him healthy? How good is he at getting people healthy? What happened in that last game? That guy got cramps. Why did that guy get cramps?*

We're working out like crazy, and he's not drinking enough fluid and not eating the right foods. Who's in charge of that? Let's make sure that happens immediately."

"Tackling the issues on and off the field is equally important to win a game and ultimately a championship." ~ **Mike Haynes**

The best part was that his teammates were constantly talking about their goal. It's not like you wait until the end of the year and then check back to see if you made it through school. They knew where they were every single game.

Similarly, in most companies, every part of a company has someone that is in charge of it. When Mike was in a highly important leadership role within the NFL, he had a person who would tell him what was going on in the league, what was going on with all the teams, who was having a good time, who was having a bad time, and most importantly why. In order to do his job well, people needed to provide Mike with feedback. He wanted to know if they needed him to adjust his performance by stepping up more or stepping down, depending on the situation. Mike needed people telling him that because at the end of the day, they all had the same goal, and they all worked very hard to achieve it as a team with their best individual contributions. Feedback and communication are essential.

"You have no chance to win a championship if not everyone has bought into the goal." ~ **Make Haynes**

In Mike's extensive experience in an NFL leadership role as a Vice President of Player and Employee Development, in addition to Special Advisor to the Commissioner of the NFL responsible for providing counsel on player issues, he made training his team a priority. Regardless of their level, he made all of his team members go through initial training and ensured that less experienced team members were learning and developing through ongoing training. As part of the training routine, Mike also challenged his team members to try something new for only 30 days. In some of his team members, he observed a major transformation occur as he had seen earlier in his life.

This was a practice that he first learned about during the time he wanted so badly to escape the LA social and economic problems that he experienced daily until he left for college. He was thinking about what he could do on his own. Initially, he felt like he couldn't do anything. But he was lucky and made it to college, and started reading books about motivation that included the insights "You are what you think you are" and "You can change your life."

As he started listening to speakers more and more, the words "Just try it for 30 days" kept ringing in his ears. After he had written these words down like one of the speakers suggested, he was ready to do it for 30 days. The key is you have got to change something immediately. So Mike changed the way he dressed so that now he looked the part as a college student. That was immediately noticed by everyone and boosted his self-confidence.

The next thing he did was practice being positive for 30 days. Every comment out of his mouth was positive. Initially, he realized how difficult that was to do. Somebody would say something like, "That coach is always picking on the such and such person." Before Mike would have had nothing to say, but now he would reply with "Maybe that coach has a different perspective that we need to take a look at."

After the 30 days, Mike was so surprised how much his words had a really large impact on others. As he reflected on these moments, he asked himself, "Is it me because I'm a leader, or is it just my words, or is it just the way that I'm feeling about things. I'm not sure, but I like what's happening." So the 30 days turned into part of a lifestyle change that would continue to impact positively the lives of others, a far cry from his childhood as an inner city kid.

After that, Mike focused on picking good friends, people whom he respected, and just sitting down and talking with them. This new mindset also required changing the friends that he already had. A lot of friends that he had were trying to bring him down. No matter how positive he was or how successful he was getting, they said that it wasn't the true him. They wanted him to be and stay the same as them. He was smart to recognize that he had to break loose of those friends to create and maintain a positive environment.

Mike takes all of his goals seriously, just like he did with his 30 day positive challenge. His current goal is to live to be 125, so health and wellness are hugely important to him. As a result, he has become an expert on stress reduction: sleeping enough, eating right, and monitoring one's lifestyle. Mike is now 62, so when he tells people that his goal is to live to 125, he also says that he's not too old to become a lawyer or a doctor.

His big WHY today is giving back to the community. He does that so well in many different ways, including as a spokesperson for the Know Your Stats (KnowYourStats.org) About Prostate Cancer Campaign. Mike is passionately committed to sharing the message of early prostate cancer detection. Mike was very lucky to detect his prostate cancer at an early stage in 2008, and he works today with the American Urology Association.

It's a huge eye opener for so many people. Why? For instance, a lot of people his age would say, "I'm headed to the golf course today." Mike recognized early that he is not cut from that same cloth and that playing only golf daily was just not for him. Instead, Mike is reprogramming himself to be something else, something greater, in fact, something exceptional. We can program ourselves to do great things and to play a bigger game – it is simply our choice.

When Mike and I discussed emotional intelligence and maturity, he was not sure how he tapped into his emotional maturity so early. It must be his upbringing and the harsh environment that he was exposed to early on in life. As a result, when Mike was in college, he selected a secondary education major. He realized that he wanted to be a school principal so that he could hire teachers who would not judge a book by its cover, and who wanted to teach kids so that they could really understand writing, reading, math, and history.

But when he found that teachers made so little money, he didn't want to be the first person in his family to make less than what his mom was making as a beautician. So he switched his major to business and finance. For Mike everything came full circle: even though he did not pursue teaching, his job in the NFL's player and employee development was similar to being a school principal. He was helping coaches educate players.

For Mike, going to college was a huge disappointment because he thought that when he got to college they were going to teach him to go out and make a difference in the world.

As a business major, he was disappointed that he wasn't taught how to start and run a business. Instead, they were teaching him how to go get a job and how to work for other people. He thought college was meant to teach you to be a free thinker. But that was not the case for him. As a father, with one of his sons going to college soon, he is looking for schools that will be teaching his son while letting him decide what he wants to be.

What is more important for Mike is the traits of individuals who are willing to take a risk, to be different, to get out there, and to say something that is controversial because it's the way they feel. Mike doesn't want conformists on his teams. He wants individuals who stand up for themselves and are accountable.

As people, we learn a lot by what we see. So by believing, likewise we can achieve something. Sometimes, the reason we are not trying to do something is because we don't think we can achieve it, and we base this decision on seeing what others are doing or not doing in our circle.

Mike learned early in life the importance of the power of the mind – both as an athlete as well as a businessman – by changing his reality and environment through meditation and visualization. He is puzzled with the fact that the mind is that powerful but wonders why someone isn't teaching us to use it that way? Why aren't more people achieving success?

"To reach success through a magnitude of team dynamics, it is essential to reach the spirit of union."
~ Izabela, The World Messenger

Take Action:

Identifying Your WHY

We all have a purpose, what is yours? Use these questions as an aid to discovering your WHY.

1. How can you make a difference in people's lives?

2. What initiative and what changes do you need to make to act out your potential?

Chapter Seven

Unearthing Your Capacity to Hope

It was the end of the summer of 2001, and I was working for a non-profit organization in Denver, Colorado focusing on rehabilitating genocide, war trauma, torture, and human trafficking survivors. My work at the non-profit was one of my most rewarding personal and professional experiences.

During my decade working with this organization, I experienced some of the most heartfelt discoveries and connections with a wide range of people from different parts of the world. They taught me the most profound and unexpected lessons in life. Through work with such a diverse group of people, I learned many universal truths and shared understandings, as well as many differences and various perspectives. Unleashing this flow of information made my life experiences and learning so much richer.

One day, I was sitting in the small room where clients often waited for their appointments while reading books or magazines on the big sofa or just watching TV. I felt sick to my stomach. I could not move for a minute, I was gasping for air. Tears where rolling down my cheeks blurring my vision, mimicking my blurred mushy mind. So many emotions bubbled in me, and in the end came a profound sadness and stone cold silence as if I was in a mortuary.

I had been asked by one of the counselors to come to the small waiting room to meet one of the clients whom I did not know well. I would see this particular client coming in occasionally to the office for private counseling sessions, but I had never talked to him or gotten to know him. The only thing I knew was that he, like I, was from the former Yugoslavia; he was originally from Serbia. This was a rather unusual request, I thought to myself as I approached the waiting room.

From underneath his big leather jacket, the client pulled out a movie and said in English, "Please watch this movie with me." His counselor nodded her head with an encouraging look on her face. At that moment I did not have any idea what the movie was about, let alone why we were going to watch it together, especially at work.

Nobody explained anything to me and as I started to ask questions, I was instead asked to, "Please, just watch," which in the end is exactly what I did.

My instincts told me that this was a bad idea but somehow, despite feeling that, I sat down and watched. Two hours flew by quickly, stirring up millions of emotions within me. I was tense, speechless, and shocked. I felt like I was in some other world, in a very different time zone.

The movie we watched was "Shot Through the Heart" and it reflected many vivid images of the horrors of the Balkan war, especially the siege of Sarajevo. It was a true story about two best friends, a Muslim and a Serb, both expert sharpshooters who ended up on opposing sides of the Bosnian War in Sarajevo. One of them became a sniper and a trainer for the Serbian Republic army. The other man became a marksman in the army of the Republic of Bosnia and Herzegovina. In the end, they face off against each other. Only one friend survives.

I started to relive the war all over again as I was watched the movie (and this lasted for weeks). My heart shattered into a million pieces while watching the movie and I didn't know if it could be whole again.

The client turned to me after the movie was over, as I sat frozen, numb, and speechless. He proceeded to tell me something very important to him that I later understood was his unbearable guilt and internal torment, the worst agony someone can have.

"Izabela," he said, I was one of the snipers in Sarajevo, in Sarajevo's Brewery, but I was forced to do it. I had just gotten married, and my wife was pregnant when a group of military guys picked me up in the middle of the night and took me away. "I was blindfolded and drugged. I woke up in the brewery and was given a rifle. My orders were to 'infuse daily fear' by killing and severely wounding many people to create a blood bath.

If I refused, they told me that they would kill my young pregnant wife and then my whole family. Trust me, I did not have a choice. Often, I would even scream 'run' to the people so I could spare them."

My heart was racing up and down and my throat was dry, very dry. I couldn't say a word. With big blue pleading eyes and with a hopeful voice he asked, "Please forgive me!"

Then it hit me. I was there so he could seek forgiveness and feel better as he had lost his soul to the devil. Tears rolled down my cheeks as I remembered in slow motion my dad, my friends, and other people who lost their lives during the war.

What could I do? What should I do?

I remembered the story of Amira and Bosko, Sarajevo's Romeo and Juliet. Both of them were killed by a sniper on their way to freedom, on the Vrbanja bridge in Sarajevo. They lay dead for seven days until their decomposing bodies were finally picked up by prisoners of war under the orders of the Bosnian Serb Army force in the middle of the night. Their story traveled the world, movies were made, books were written, and their case was never solved.

What should I say?

Somehow, slowly, I managed to nod my head. Weakly, I whispered, "Yes."

That day, I stayed in the office longer than usual, collecting my thoughts and finding the strength to drive home. I somehow finally left and managed to wander to my favorite escape, Overlook Mountain. There I gazed outward at millions of lights in the city as I searched inward for answers that I already instinctively knew.

I never saw that man again. He and his wife left Colorado and went underground. In the meantime, I did my very best to continue my work as usual.

In my work, I faced many moral, ethical, legal, professional, and personal dilemmas. I am not ready to share all of these dilemmas, nor how I handled them. I can say my thoughts and actions were never about revenge or hate – but were always about allowing ourselves to see both sides of the coin before we make decisions or judgment calls, before we react. It is about having hope that others will learn to know the "what" and "why" of their actions. In the same time, it is about allowing ourselves to learn a different point of view and have, as much as possible, a 360 degree overview. You may be surprised by what you can learn.

Before I could fully shake off the effects of meeting the sniper and seeing the movie, the September 11th attack occurred. The level of chaos, pain, blame, confusion, frustration, anger, and disbelief started to turn into rage and open hate. Some of that hate was so public, shameful, and unnecessary. The hate created harm and separation, impacting the support and unity in the country I now called home. In a very short time, I saw the worst, most horrible, and ugliest acts and comments made based on this hate, this pure ignorance, and fear.

Again, there are the two sides of the coin that we often don't see at all or as a whole. Miracles started unfolding, many of them warming my heart with hope. At the same time that I saw hate, I saw profound human compassion and support that touched me so deeply, making me feel that I am part of a society that values and appreciates good people, regardless of where they may come from.

Living with both sides of the coin, experiencing the mix of emotions, there were times when I found myself in a big black hole, a pit that reminded me once again why I do what I do and what I should do next. I started to serve more and more, staying at work longer, involving myself in community activities on evenings and weekends as my way to show solidarity, support, and my Super Powers – hoping that everything would be fine.

*"A warm smile is the universal language of kindness, as is a
warm hug, the universal language of compassion."*
~ Izabela, The World Messenger

I felt more deep sadness as clients came to the center and shared
their concerns for their safety on the streets, in their schools, and
overall in the Denver community. Some of them felt so scared as if
they were in a war zone all over again, because they could be easily
identified by their ethnic clothing and heavy accents. Some of them
had a hard time gaining or keeping employment as low-paying jobs
were affected by the changing economy and different employer
preferences. It was painful to watch. It was heartbreaking.

*When people start to learn how to think, access, process, and
utilize information on their own, many start to create success. The key
point of change was when they started to feel unconditional love and
feel empowered to take action as well as control of their own lives. For
some people this may be their first such experience even though they
were already well into their adulthood.*

During those first months after September 11th I was involved
in building strategic partnerships and alliances to support the
immigrant and refugee population in Colorado. I was deeply touched
by how many organizations and businesses, with their leadership
teams, stepped up beyond what was expected or asked for. These
groups included a wide range of faith-based congregations.

In moments like those, my heart blossomed, not only helping me to
redefine hope within myself but also within the clients I was helping
and serving. One of the biggest compliments and validations of my
service during this time came from a sweet, wise Sufi Master. His
words kept me going beyond my days at the non-profit organization.
He looked me straight in the eyes with his smiling, calming face.
While holding my hands, he said, *"You are the girl that helped us to
restore our dreams."*

His words gave me a deeper sense of meaning, renewed purpose, and a new tie to hope. This was the first time I took a step back to reflect how my words and actions directly impacted the people I helped. I wanted to determine what specific actions I had taken from helping people go from fear to greatness. I had unearthed my capacity to hope.

The more I spoke with people, especially experts in the coaching and counseling world, the more I got the same answer: hope is not only an emotion, but it is also about a process. Ok, then what kind of process?

Hope is a deep warm and fuzzy feeling. It is also a combination of setting goals that we think we can reach, combined with tenacity and perseverance. Hope is a way of thinking that we learn over time. It is like any other cognitive process that we learn in the environments that we are exposed to.

Truth be told, some things will take more effort or time and some less. Some we will enjoy more and some we will dread, some will be fun and joyful rides, while others will challenge us more than ever. Either way, we should be prepared, stay focused, hopeful, and push through.

The opposite of hope is that we often feel disappointed, discouraged, and powerless. As soon as you recognize any of these or similar feelings know that YOU, only you, hold the key to the solution as well as to the problem. My hope is that you will choose HOPE!

"HOPE = Happy, Optimistic, Perfectly Empowered YOU!"
~ Izabela, The World Messenger

I decided to attend a human rights event and co-curate the exhibit on Sarajevo and Grbavica in the memory of the lost lives during the Balkan war that occurred in Sarajevo in 2007. I felt that I had to do this, to not only find peace in my heart,but also to help others find a safe place for healing and rebuilding trust in their new multiethnic community. In order to do that, it had to start with me.

For so long, I felt like I was caught under a wave and as soon I tried to catch my breath, another wave would come. But as many times as I would fall down to my knees, I just couldn't give up. It was never an option for me.

These events that occurred while I worked at the center made me realize just how important positive thinking was and how powerful a positive mindset was, particularly when I was dragged down by the ghosts of the past who tried to sidetrack me while on my journey.

Years later, as I was sitting in Paris, in the garden at the Headquarters of the French Tennis Federation, I was reflecting on many pivotal events in my life. Big sigh!

As I was warming my body with an aromatic cappuccino and my heart with delicious dark chocolate croissants in the early morning, for the moment, time stopped. Sunshine was glistening on the leaves of flowers with their raindrops from the night before while professional players were practicing and warming up to seize their day at the Rolando Garros, the French Open tennis tournament.

My dear friend Pierre-Emmanuel Czaja, a former professional French player, reminded me about the importance to never give up and keep hope strong even when we are defeated numerous times in life. He smiled warmly, as he shared with me his profound words of wisdom.

His professional career as a young tennis player finished faster than it started. He was perfectly built for professional tennis and had tremendous potential. He was young and eager to perform. From the very beginning, he was the best he could be and had very high personal expectations. He found the coach, or better yet, the coach found him to get him on the right track.

But what Pierre did not know was that his coach had a double life, one in the Spotlight of media as a reputable professional coach, and the other one as an underground mafia leader. He played professionally only for a little over the year, and as soon as he found out with whom he was indirectly associated, his world and dreams crashed. He got scared and left France. He avoided competitions, the spotlight and started a new life in Spain. Since then, he turned himself into a serial entrepreneur who started so many new businesses, some extremely successful and lucrative, and some, through unpredictable waves of the global economy, left him financially broke.

But deep down he knew that he couldn't just give up, even in the moments when he did not have anything of value to claim in his name. The reality is that even in the worst moments of his life, he knew that he still had so much going for him. Many valuable life experiences, knowledge, and learning over time got him again to the top-as a winning champion.

As we shared and compared some of our pivotal moments while enjoying Paris, he reminded me of the power of the butterfly effect. I smiled. I silently remembered that a seemingly minor single event in one location can influence and can change the course of the universe forever later on. It gave me a new sense of hope that it may not be evident at that moment that, the chaos in our lives, specific situations, and conditions can change for the better in time to come.

Pierre is the perfect example of how an exceptional path of personal growth and success can be driven by hope. Today, he launched Setteo (www.setteo.com), a unique, ambitious and innovative social network dedicated exclusively to racket sports. His love and passion for tennis is offering the world so much more through this interactive and innovative social platform. These results would have been impossible for him to accomplish without his unearthing hope and starting all over again. This time, a new start with great friends, partnerships and alliances.

"Why play alone when we can play together!"
~ Pierre-Emmanuel Czaja

Another powerful glimpse of hope came through my South African friend and colleague, Warwick Bashford. He is like a cat with nine lives who has endured so much while discovering his hope in the worst moments of defeat and life challenges. Today, he is a transformational coach focusing on Tennis Mental Toughness while building The Championship Mindset among professional tennis players.

But before he got where he is today, he lived in a very hard environment in South Africa. He started to think about his emotional motivation to get out of the situation he was in while living in South Africa. He used his passion for sports, specifically tennis and his tennis racket as a passport for a better life. He decided at a specific moment at 14 years old, that nothing is going to stop him from achieving his goal: a better quality of life. But the path was rocky and very challenging. He was the kid with the accent, a foreigner everywhere he would go, an easy target for kids to make fun of and give him a hard time.

"The only time to look back in life, is to gain inspiration to go forward." **~ Warwick Bashford**

His emotional motivation continued even in the times of profound emotional and physical pain. At those moments, Warwick fueled his internal fire through his tennis racket and hours of practice. At numerous times, unearthing his hope, he realized how important it was for him to transcend his ego in order to succeed in his personal and professional life. Like me, he was an early bloomer and we were both unlike the numerous professional athletes and business people that stayed in the self-centered, "all about me" ego-driven mindset. He had to learn how to deal with this type of personality. Truth be told, this was not an easy task for either one of us growing up.

"If you are discontent and do not change direction, you may end up going nowhere." ~ **Warwick Bashford**

Sadly, many people are afraid to show who they truly are so that others can't "see" or discover their real thought process or weakness. They hide and pretend. In the end, they can't reach their true potential nor achieve the results they are hoping or capable of reaching. Some of them live in pain, often self-inflicted. In my years of professional counseling, consulting and coaching experience, this type of pain is the worst one to deal with yet the easiest to cure.

Even the strongest pain will fade away – eventually.

"You are made with the most outstanding ability to rebuild, recover, regroup, and revive yourself and your life!"
~ **Izabela, The World Messenger**

Take Action:

Unearthing Your Capacity to Hope

In difficult situations finding positivity can be challenging. I challenge you to find hope within you and remember to use it, with the help of these questions.

1. When did you lose hope and why?

2. What steps can you take to prevent losing hope?

3. What can you do to remind yourself to not lose hope?

Chapter Eight

Getting Back Up On Your Path to Freedom

Reflecting back on the many powerful interviews with professional athletes and coaches from around the world, I found one more common thread between all of us, including business leaders and influencers.

Regardless of whether we are a champion in sports, business, or life, we all require passion, drive, and a competitive champion spirit.

At some point in our life, all of us have felt that we are warriors, fighting our own battles. The battles can be in schools, in relationships, in business, in sports, you name it. The core principles of self-discipline, focus, and need to influence the crowd are common across the board for both male and female leaders. Some of us fail and get back up quickly, and others struggle for a long time to find and achieve a new path.

The difference is that some of us had to fight for our life, the injustice that put us, with force, in the arena. And as a result, we truly need to find the path to freedom quickly. Otherwise we may perish. As in my case, in a war torn county similar to millions of others across the globe. For some, this may be just a metaphor or perception during daily escapes from day-to-day life. Some of us may choose to participate in it without knowing our opponent, fearlessly. And some of us may be at the wrong time at the wrong place, or simply needed to learn a specific lesson.

As for the warrior's arena, it is a new world where he or she spends significant amounts of time – battling. Today, each one of us performs in our own arena, beyond Roman and Greek times of fights that influenced one of the oldest sports – Greco-Roman wrestling, a sport in my mind that represents the Olympic Games. Talk about a tradition that is dated way back when, right?

Battles during the time of warriors had sets of rules and specific boundaries, often hidden or invisible; likewise, as do our "battles" today. To master these battles, we need to be more than ever present and aware. What are your arenas today? Where and how well do you perform? Are you making an impact? Are you making a positive impact? Why? Why not? How are you "battling?" Do you even have to "battle?" What is the battle all about?

It is essential to be honest with ourselves if we are to be successful. Just as each sport has its own set of rules and guidance for best practices, business has them too. The arena for the small entrepreneur may be quite different than the arena of the executive negotiating his or her path through an analysis and matrix driven organization.

The key is to know the rules, because if the rules are ignored, then it is an open invitation for a wide range of issues. I am talking about, wrong moves, shortcuts that kill our reputation and trust through manipulation, poor performance, betrayal or gossip. As a result, people often choose to change the arena they are in by replacing it with something more manageable or easier to agree with, or something less frightening, or more appealing.

> *"The game is always on regardless if you are in it or on the sidelines, regardless of whether you are ready or not."*
> ~ **Izabela, The World Messenger**

So many of you and those before you tried at some point to escape an arena and seek your solitude. Interestingly even when you seek to escape the games of life and choose only to meditate, it is in itself a game that you play with yourself. So you can't escape the game – it is indeed always on – in either your personal or professional life. To move forward and build momentum in playing the best game you can play, with the highest performance and impact, you have to accept your chosen arena, welcome it with open arms, and determine wholeheartedly to be the most successful warrior that you can be.

I am not suggesting killing, cheating, tricking, lying, manipulating, betraying, playing with, and seducing others.

I am not suggesting that you start another war or conflict to divide and conquer new territories. Just as it was hard throughout ancient time to gain victory and support of the crowd, today it may appear to be the same. You must be wondering then how do you succeed? Is it even possible? Is it the same success formula today as it was back then? You succeed by winning people's hearts, affection, and ongoing support. By facing adversity with courage, by the ability to take a hit without giving up, and by continuing to fight until the very end, however long that may be.

> *"You succeed by winning people's hearts, affection, and ongoing support!"* ~ Izabela, The World Messenger

I am suggesting you select your unique positive "fighting" style to play the best game of life that you can. Back in ancient times, some warriors fought with very limited tools such as a spear or a sword while others with sword and shield. Today, you have so much more to choose from to get you to achieve our greatest path to freedom and beyond. Each one of you has unique gifts and talents, different ways of communicating, behaving, or relating to each other.

That is so powerful! As a result, you should be able to identify if you are using you best style to produce the best results for you. Many of you do not have a clue what the best style is for you, let alone how to master "my style." You cannot adapt your style when you are not even given an opportunity to give your best effort for getting desirable results.

> *"The one who goes the extra mile to reach his or her goal, is the true champion of them all."* ~ Izabela, The World Messenger

This is where self-realization, knowledge, and development come into play, including self-leadership. The fact is that there is nothing more rewarding and more magnificent than being better than your former self. That is when you indeed break free.

But if you are afraid to talk about your challenges and obstacles, or even acknowledge that they exist, you will not be learning and getting stronger as you need to in order to reach your maximum potential.

More than ever, it is important to acknowledge and appreciate people of significance in your life, your true supporters, cheerleaders, mentors, friends, parents, partners, and anyone else who stood and continues to stand by your side through your biggest and longest struggle – your life.

I am talking about reaching your greatness through the brave warrior heart that you have inside of you. Perhaps you are not aware of your warrior's heart because fear hides it. True greatness cannot be reached in fear. It can be reached by conquering fear. It is time for you to claim the power of the warrior within. It is a time for you to claim your power within. It is your time to be a true warrior!

"True greatness cannot be reached in fear. It can only be reached by conquering fear!" ~ **Izabela, The World Messenger**

At the end of the day, success is up to you and your desire to be the best. On this journey of getting back up and carving your path to freedom, I share with you Merril Hoge's journey. I took an interest in Merril and selected him for the book because of the powerful story behind his success. For you who don't know who he is, Merril is a former professional American football player who played as a running back for the Pittsburgh Steelers and Chicago Bears. Today, he is a fiery football analyst for ESPN television.

Merril is the first one to tell you that nothing in life comes risk free. The question is what risks are we willing to take? The sooner that we accept that, the sooner we can get ready for the amazing ride called life. By eliminating unwanted risks such as fear, toxic dependencies, unhealthy relationships, and abuse, we can achieve freedom.

Why is it important for you to achieve your path to freedom? It will set you free from all those inner demons so that you can be free to reach your true potential.

"Football was my dream regardless of challenges I had to face!"
~ Merril Hoge

If you have never played professional sports, you may be surprised about how much commitment is required to do your job well, in fact, to do your job the best that you can. It is a constant battle; work is required all the time. Merril is the first one to tell you that as a result of pressure and high demands as a professional player he had to take a road less traveled.

"My love and passion for the game and being on the stage kept
me to be and stay focused." ~ Merril Hoge

That attitude of love and passion for the game and being on the stage led him to stay focused and reach success in sports as well as in life and business. It felt in a way that he was preparing himself for the biggest game in his life, one that was yet to come. And indeed it did. Instead of the football field, it came in the hospital. In fact, it led him to claim the biggest victory in his whole life by beating the gloomy diagnosis and prognosis of cancer.

"When I had to face cancer and 'red death' chemo, I knew I had
to stay on track with my plan ..." Merril shared a glimpse of how he succeeded despite the doctor's prognosis. During his cancer treatment, he played basketball every day. Playing basketball was the best thing he did for himself. He would drink one to two gallons of water every day after chemo, pushing himself through the worst kind of pain he had to face. On the basketball court, he would sweat like crazy so all the toxic chemicals that he got during the chemo treatment would leave his body within less than 24 hours.

This was when he tapped into mental and emotional toughness like never before. I asked him why.

According to Merril, *"My big WHY were my kids – my biggest motivation and will power to live for them. I lost my mom very young, and I did not want them to live without a parent."* He shared this as he reflected on the moments of the terrible pain that he was able to successfully manage and ultimately defeat. What an amazing spirit of the true Warrior he is.

I also love this part of self-discovery that he shared with me. A vital element in addition to his mental and emotional toughness, the spiritual toughness, his faith that he uses for winning in sports, business, and life. In fact, he shared with me with pride that his *"tool belt comes with mental, emotional, and spiritual strength."*

"Vital element for winning in sports, business, and life: Strong Faith!" ~ Merril Hoge

He would always push as far he could, playing his part with his team, his friends, or his family. He would even challenge others by asking them, "Did you do your part?" It was simple – if you did, then you had nothing to worry about and that makes a whole lot of a difference. In my ears his profound statement still echoes: "I have great faith in the outcome once I have done my part!" He can indeed teach us what that means in any aspect of our lives.

"I have great faith in the outcome once I have done my part!" ~ Merril Hoge

During our conversation I just could not resist asking him about the story of his short ties, for those of you who know who he is, you understand my curiosity. He told me that as a kid he wore a belt buckle and wanted others to see it. He started to tie his ties so that they were short, and before he knew it, it became his thing. He is even recognized as Mr. Short Tie by some. His story reminded me of my week as the sheriff in town back in my teens.

Merril hopes to be remembered by "the legacy of a genuine person, a good dad, a teammate, and player.

Someone who is giving back by paying forward, in addition to writing a new book on parenting and coaching."

"People are like art: Sometimes we look closely and see so much; sometimes we miss what's in front of us and see only emptiness."
~ Izabela, The World Messenger

Many professionals on LinkedIn reacted to this quote after their interpretation and coming from their unique point of view. Like anything in life, it all depends on the lens or the world-view that we are looking through at the specific moment in time. Nothing is permanent, everything is changing as well as our perspective.

What I found to echo further than anything else is love, like fear, is in the eye of the beholder – the choice is always ours. The universe that we are surrounded with is mostly empty, offering us the opportunity to see, feel, and experience its rich emptiness. This takes us a step closer to self-realization, self-discovery and understanding what role and how we choose to play.

It is essential that we learn how to look outside our immediate perceptions and surroundings if we want to accomplish something exceptional and revolutionary. During Henry Ford's innovative era, he shared something very profound, "If I had asked the people what they wanted, they would have said faster horses." Instead, he created cars that replaced the limited perception of transportation solutions at that time. Look where we are today as a result of his vision. Sometimes, we are the only ones that hold the vision of something profound that is yet to come. Thus, it is so important to persevere regardless of how long or challenging our path may be.

We are living as humans in a highly complex world, while we are the most complicated of creatures still searching for millions of answers not only about ourselves but others too. Be determined to do your part to build strong faith within you. Spend your time wisely, with positive and uplifting towards people – things will start unfolding much faster for you.

Disrupt your daily routine, your day in general and your way of thinking. You may be surprised about what could happen next.

This is how a big a-ha moment unfolded for me recently. It was a Wednesday, middle of the week with an unexpected break. My great friend, Scott Palat, who I often reference as my brother, invited me to take a hike and asked me to do a photo shoot of him for his marketing needs. It was one of the most glorious mornings in Evergreen, Colorado. The night before we got fresh snow and the evergreen trees were covered in fluffy white snow appearing so festive and magical. I had a million things going through my mind, feeling overwhelmed and honestly a little bit lost – where to go, what to do next, thinking how behind I would get if I left home – that nudging voice telling me to focus on my work and just stay home. But I refused.

In midst of the chaos in my mind, I knew that going for a hike and helping Scott was the right thing to do in my gut and I pushed all of the possible negativity creeping into my consciousness telling me otherwise. Even my dog, Jack, looked at me with the most guilt tripping, adorable face as I was leaving without him. I was so excited to see Scott and help him. He is one of the nicest guys you will ever meet, always happy, positive, and willing to assist. He is a big dreamer and visionary leader like myself so when we get together, we ignite a buzzing energy.

Despite the ice, snow, and bumps on the side roads, my SUV ride to meet up with Scott was starting to distract me from my initial negative thoughts. My spirits lifted when I saw his smiling, positive face at his home warmly greeting me. Scott is a serial entrepreneur who has had astonishing results as an internet marketer, and he is so willing to help others to replicate and duplicate his success. He even went as far as creating results focused accountability software that allows him and others to guarantee success for their clients and train the perfect employees.

As we were driving around and stopping to take perfect shots of the majestic morning, we laughed and played like kids while we talked lightly about the very next best idea. He had an surprise for me – he was taking me to Mount Vernon Country Club for lunch. My day was just getting better each minute since I had stepped out of my regular schedule of consulting work and took time just for me. To be honest, this felt like a different type of luxury since I do work on things I love every single day.

As we were sitting in the large dining room with the most spectacular views of the mountain ranges and above the clouds, I was lost for the moment in my daydreaming. I felt an overwhelming feeling of deep gratitude that I was able to enjoy that moment of gorgeous nature, great friendship, and good food.

I shifted my gears to neutral after not having done so for a long, long time. I was coasting on Cloud Nine. And reflecting. At that moment, I reflected on the last three years of my life, which had been so intense. I lost my mom and aunt, both to the cancer battle, in addition to several friends. I then also lost my loving grandmother, the last mentor and rock in my life. I was devastated. I was on my own during these losses, offering support to others while I was stuffing my sorrows, sadness, and suffering deep down. These changes were monumental in my life.

Many times during this period of loss, I would lay on my bed in a little ball, wondering if the pain in my chest would ever get better, lighter, and eventually completely disappear. I prayed to survive one more day to the next – the best coping mechanism that I had. I was able to be strong in the public eye and with family, but in my own personal world – I felt that somehow everything was falling apart.

"To move forward, you have to re-think your thinking! By knowing how to think versus what to think, you can solve anything and be the best version of you!"
~ Izabela, The World Messenger

What I learned during this time about myself is true that what does not kill you – indeed makes you stronger and prepares you for something bigger in life. I went through this experience fully alone. My closest friends were going through their issues and could not relate to me in the ways I was hoping. In those moments, I never felt so broken and alone.

But, I knew that I was alive for a reason and that I had to keep moving. I started to make progress in parts of my life that I could celebrate as small victories or miracles, and then things started unfolding faster so that I could continue building up momentum on my path to freedom.

"If it is a wrong or unnecessary thing to do, who cares how well you can do it. You are wasting your two most precious assets: time and energy!"
~ Izabela, The World Messenger

Never underestimate yourself and the perfect timing in your life that will take you on the path to freedom to achieve greatness. It can come through in so many unexpected ways.

Take for example the path many Iraqi athletes maneuvered through to become Olympians; sadly, for many it was not towards freedom. Through contact with the USA Olympic Community from Colorado Springs, I was able to speak with a wrestling Olympic coach from Iraq seeking support during one of the hardest moments of his life. This was a heart-wrenching situation. Quickly I found myself on an emotional and mental rollercoaster ride.

The brutality perpetrated on the Iraqi people during Saddam's regime was unspeakable, especially for athletes. Consequences were awful if they would lose a game or not perform to the level of satisfaction of Saddam's son Uday, who was the head of Iraq's Olympic committee.

Uday's disturbed version of motivation and coaching was threatening players with torture if they lost the game or if they performed poorly. Weirdly, if they performed well and would get more attention from the fans more than Uday got, they could be punished again. Sadly, he started torturing members of the Olympic wrestling team. Some of them survived the brutality but were scarred permanently, some of them ran away, and some of them lost their lives during the horrors of Uday's sadistic beatings and torture.

Through everything, there was this coach who was loving and caring, even if those characteristics were forbidden during Saddam Hussein's regime in Iraq. The coach was brave with strong faith that even during the worst oppression they experienced in Iraq he kept coaching, cheering and supporting his team. Even through small activities in a damaged building, improvising exercises he kept as much as possible players morale and faith strong.

He gave me a new meaning of heart – not as an organ that pumps blood, but the depth of human emotions to do what you love and care for even if that meant possible execution or prosecution. He was one of the lucky ones that escaped the country right after training and preparation for a big tournament. But sadly, his wife and a newborn son were left behind as was most of his team. He tormented himself every single day feeling survivor's guilt and constant worry for his loved ones, friends, and teammates.

After prescreening and assessing over 5,000 of torture, war trauma, human trafficking and genocide survivors first hand, this was a new way to see personal grit, with highly developed resilience and strength. It just does not happen overnight. This level of determination is so rare to see. But under special conditions and through major change and vulnerability, it can lead to profound personal transformation.

As I reflect back and recall this moment in time, I realize that for each person going through the most challenging events in their life, the initial objective is to survive, to just get through it.

It is like setting your goal to finish a marathon no matter how long it takes, what storms you may weather or how much effort or energy it will take to do it. For many of us, this is like completing the end exam or finishing that long, painful run.

"When you are going through the most unspeakable and challenging events in your life, your initial objective is to 'just get through it." ~ Izabela, The World Messenger

To get back up and get on your path to freedom, regardless what you might be experiencing, it is essential to have your tool belt on you to endure and overcome during times of challenge. The only difference is that you maybe don't have the mental, physical, emotional, or spiritual tools or equipment to get you to practice or even train over a specific time. Often, like we do in life, we find ourselves in the middle of feeling overwhelmed – with a huge task or objective still to accomplish. This in a way is like seeing only a big elephant that you have to conquer. So many times we keep hearing, "How do you eat an elephant?" without even thinking we know the answer, intuitively we know, it is one bite at the time, right?

This is exactly how we overcome our biggest challenges and how we reach our biggest goals – through consistent, small efforts over a period of time. So many people think that by occasionally doing one big thing it will speed the process or get us faster to where we need or want to be. Some even think by inviting additional people to the effort that the large group will decrease the effort needed. This may work somewhat in very rare occasions, but you still have to do your own work. Cutting corners will not get you far – the decision is still yours to make though.

You can't win championships without practicing. You can't be the best version of you if you live your life by chance – it has to be a conscious effort – that is the only way to make it happen. The key is to recognize and then accept your own vulnerability and to be okay with that. And then do the work!

Take Action:

Getting Back Up On Your Path to Freedom

I invite you to consider the following questions to help you determine what to do to free yourself from whatever is holding you back. Note: Consider incorporating your answers from Chapter One.

1. When you have been knocked down, what have you done to get back up?

2. What can you do to empower yourself to achieve your dream(s)?

Chapter Nine

Believing Within & In Unseen Forces

The power of belief is attainable yet reached by few during the most challenging moments in life. It propels us or prevents us from fulfilling our potential based on our mindset. People with a growth based mindset can achieve the highest levels of achievement because of their willingness to embrace change and persist while facing setbacks. While this is applicable to all aspects of life, it is especially true with sports because so many people are invested in a positive outcome. Sports play a key role in education, health, and social growth.

I found sports to be one of the biggest metaphors for life. By looking closely into sports, we can see lessons that apply in every aspect of our life, from relationships and families to teams and companies. Can you possibly imagine discussing the world without thoughts from sports? I can't! It would be impossible. We think about the world and how it works through sports metaphors of healthy competitions, challenges, conflicts, and at times struggles, tensions, even breakthroughs, victories, and triumphs.

The sport itself is based on the ability to merge pride and prejudice, heart and intellect, emotion and talent, passion and drive. Sports have a dynamic to be examined and learned from. Lessons from sports offer a hidden power to become, to grow, and to transform an entire nation and the world from spectators to united for a cause. That is powerful, isn't it?

Think about how you can apply this hidden power within you. The great news is that each one of us has that power within ourselves, that juice, the irresistible, hidden, believing power. The power that is waiting to be unleashed to become, to grow, and to transform into the most powerful force on the planet earth. It is easy to get trapped in an overwhelming feeling of doubt, guilt, shame, unworthiness, or fear by disconnecting from the source of that amazing energy within you. These directions can be due to excruciating experiences of pain and hurt that we experience early on in our life. But what often happens by continuing to allow ourselves to be excluded from that energy and zest for life? We prevent ourselves from becoming the best version of ourselves, but also less likely to do things that we are meant to do. Believing in yourself is exemplified by the legendary Roberto Clemente. Sadly, Roberto Clemente was killed in a plane crash that was delivering relief supplies to Nicaragua in 1972, way before I was even born.

"Any time you have an opportunity to make a difference in this world and you don't, then you are wasting your time on Earth."
~ Roberto Clemente

I wish I could have met him, but I was more than fortunate to meet his son, Roberto Clemente, Jr. I must say that it was a genuine privilege to spend some time with Roberto. I felt like a five year old girl with eyes full of wonder all over again.

Roberto's dad was one of the first Hispanic players in major league baseball (MLB). He was one of the best players in baseball at that time, in fact, he is one of the best players of all time. As a European transplant, I did not know a lot about baseball until I started to get involved with the organization, The Brunch Ricky Award. Their mission is to help at-risk kids, often identified as inner-city kids. During my rich conversation with Roberto about his father, he shared so many great insights. I have broken it down into four nuggets, so you can not only discover but start fully utilizing that amazing power within you.

#1: Sense of Purpose – After the earth shattering introduction of Jackie Robinson to baseball, both Branch Rickey and Roberto Clemente knew that the player on the field could blaze another new path on the road less traveled. Roberto Clemente had to not only adjust to the pressure of proving himself to his teammates, but also to the rest of the world.Why? He was one of few men of color playing the sport at that time. Branch Rickey knew that deep in his heart that it was a time to change that by allowing other previously excluded players to compete with other athletes based on their talents, true skills, and potential, not based on their skin color.

#2: Sense of Urgency – It has been said that Roberto Clemente knew deep down that his life would be cut short. As a result, he wanted to do as much as possible with the time he had, fearlessly working on his cause and true purpose beyond playing baseball.

He lived his personal and professional role by serving others, by building strategic partnerships and alliances, giving voice to the voiceless, and building local, national, and global communities. He was also a father of three sons and a husband. He impacted many nations and people around the world by showing what is possible. He indeed created new paths to so many uncharted territories positively influenced others to follow.

#3: Profound Passion – Roberto Clement gave everything on the field and gave back to the community. He had an undying passion to serve and help others, which was consistently demonstrated by this legendary leader. His passion translated into one of the most powerful forces, known as love. But when things got so hard on and off the field for Clemente, he also had to tap into additional force, unwavering faith.

Deep down, he knew that there was a bigger reason for all the hate, racial remarks, and attacks by many Caucasian teammates as well as by spectators. He knew that he had to "fight" his war in a different way than his attackers, to win. And he was so right in his approach. The game of baseball has never been the same since then, impacting how we look at all sports today.

During the hardest moments of defeat when there was so much pain to bear, he also knew that he couldn't give up. At those moments his WHY was bigger than the world, it was echoing through the whole universe! **Get up, show up, and do your best** – it was this mantra that Clemente lived by every single day. As a result, his extraordinary legacy was born way before his deadly airplane crash.

#4: Far-Reaching Dreams – Roberto Clemente proved that dreams transcended professional sports, race, class, or economic equality! The dream of a peaceful world and its positive global impact on everyone was a key driver for many of his extraordinary actions. He had to very often believe in himself first before others started to follow, like Branch Ricky and other Pittsburgh Pirate's teammates and fans. Building more self-confidence and persistence was essential to his success. Also, Roberto Clemente was able to hold onto his vision and far-reaching dreams that he indeed accomplished during his short life.

He was an All-Star player and a Gold Glove winner for twelve seasons. He was the first Latin American and Caribbean player to win a World Series as a starter (1960), to receive the National League Most Valuable Player (1966), and to receive a World Series Most Valuable Player Award (1971). He also reached 3,000 hits, making him only the 11th player in the baseball history to reach that status. Wow! Through his professional career and his outstanding accomplishments, Roberto Clemente stayed focused, consistent, and humble while thinking about his next move, next result, and next accomplishment. He also stayed a dreamer, thinking of new ideas every day and new ways to do more for others, do something better and greater that would make a difference.

> *"Why does everyone talk about the past? All that counts is tomorrow's game."* ~ **Roberto Clemente**

In the end, it is hard not to think what he would do next, during tomorrow's game either on the baseball field or in the community. He was a role model to many families in the US and his native Puerto Rico. He was a hero to Latin Americans and those in the Caribbean community as well. He worked non-stop off the baseball field, collecting and delivering baseball equipment, medical supplies, and food to those in need. He brought much needed business at that time to underdeveloped islands, so that local people could find ways to not only survive but also to thrive over the years.

He was an excellent businessman too. Many big name popular American franchises would not have found new and successful growth opportunities if they had not had someone of his stature assist them to navigate local culture and laws.

Sadly, his life ended too soon in an aviation accident at the end of 1972 while he was delivering aid to earthquake victims in Nicaragua. Leaving his wife and three little sons so abruptly, with so many unfinished businesses, it left them without knowing what financial resources they may have to move forward. It was hard for Clemente Jr. and his brothers to help their grieving mom and to fully understand what took place the first several years after his death.

They missed their dad so much and, over time, they had to accept the fact that daddy was never coming home again. The boys were lucky to be raised by their own "Mother Teresa," their mom, Vera. She kept their dad's spirit for caring for other people in all three of his boys through their upbringing alive. Mom Vera made sure that the kids were showered with love, and support, and steeped in their dad's legacy.

What touched me so deeply during our conversation is the fact that they lost so much with the tragic death of their dad. Even though they had so little at that time, they continued to give to others. They were determined to carry out their dad's dreams, inspiring them to be better men by trying harder every single day.

> *"No matter how much we lost, we just continue to give."*
> **~ Roberto Clemente, Jr.**

These words hit close to home, especially during my first years as a refugee. Even when I had only a little, it was still something, and compared to people who had nothing, I simply just wanted to give. As you are reading this, please consider what you are giving back or wish to give back, how, and to whom. There is no better time than now!

Through my work at a non-profit organization in Denver, Colorado whose mission is to provide rehabilitative services to genocide, war trauma, human trafficking, and torture survivors, I had a chance to hear so many first hand stories of survival. Often, their stories had never been previously shared with anyone else, especially their family members. Because they wanted to avoid embarrassment, shame, guilt, and perhaps further humiliation depending on the culture that they came from.

I was deeply touched that we were able to create a safe space to generate a connection and trust between us. As a result, the sharing of stories could occur and the process begun to assist them in the most beneficial way – emotional healing. In addition, this was in most cases a first opportunity of letting go of their painful past. How liberating that felt for so many of them. After that, they were better able to progress with new challenges in their life by discovering once again a new sense of purpose and belief within themselves.

This was when I understood a wide range of emotions in a completely new way, beyond data, research, theories, algorithms, statistics, charts, and numbers. The fact is that all of us have the capacity not only to feel and experience a spectrum of negative as well as positive emotions, but also the ability to recognize those emotions in others. And if we are willing, we have the ability to help others out.

After looking deeply into the eyes and faces of "I am not good enough or worthy of..." I started to see patterns and common threads. So many people are simply uncomfortable in their own skin and feel that they are not good enough or not deserving for good and positive things to happen in their life. Some of them never experienced "good." That made me so sad to see way too often, especially in the community of youth and young adults I encountered through my numerous high school and college speaking engagements and interventions.

Often, we hit rock bottom, feeling so miserable that we do not know what to do. I see this pattern way too often, and it pains me knowing that each one of us can make better choices. I see more people operating in fear and lack of self-belief and confidence in this country of endless opportunities and resources. I see that in so many faces at work cafeterias, business offices, waiting rooms, grocery stores, airports, hotels, and even on the streets – I see it everywhere.

I see it on first dates, job interviews, first meetings with a new team member or potential friends. People are trying so hard to prove themselves or be someone or something else that they simply are not. So many people are working so hard to be liked, accepted, and loved while using the wrong methods and approaches, sometimes even going too far due to pure desperation. Some, simply so emotionally shot down, look like a blank canvas or a dark cloud.

We have access to everything, but so many people make wrong choices. Some think that shortcuts or manipulation will do. It usually doesn't work in the long run because it can't be sustained. You will learn that lesson eventually, hopefully before you need things to work out the most. In fact, all of us at some point in our lives have criticized ourselves and have been criticized by others, and this made us stronger or weaker. But over time we learned that we have a choice of who and what we want to be. Deep inside yourself you know what kind of person you are meant to be. Think like the person you are meant to become.

I had the opportunity to meet and talk to in person with Price Pritchett, Ph.D., an excellent business advisor, speaker, and author. He is a pioneer in mergers and acquisition (M&A), integration strategies, and organizational culture and change, especially with a focus on change management. His track record is exceptional. Price has sold thus far over 12 million M&A and change management books and trained more people in M&A integration than anyone else.

As you can imagine, change is not only a personal struggle for so many of us on an individual level but also in our working environments too. The fact that over five thousand companies have used Price's change management training to mobilize their organization for successful change tells you a lot about how we struggle as humans with regards to change. I am sharing this with you because you need to believe within yourself that you can and want to change so that you will change.

Further, I hope that you will soon recognize that change is a good thing, in fact a great thing if you ask me. It will help you to stay current with your skill set at work before you and your position become obsolete. It will help you with your friends and family, especially in your personal relationship because you will be more adaptable and resilient to change too. And in a sport, a good dose of change or willingness to try new things in a new way, just may give you that extra edge to get you from a good athlete to a great one!

"If you must doubt something, doubt your limits." ~ Price Pritchett

Recently I also spoke with executives from two different prominent consulting firms. Not only did both senior executives recognize a need for change internally within their departments but also within their organization as a whole. During our extensive conversation, I was surprised also to receive feedback that I had not expected, but very much welcomed. Both of them in as many words thought about me as a poster child of change on a personal level as well as professionally. They could clearly see me delivering effective and customized change management that could quickly tailor to customer needs.

I was not surprised to hear that assessments, concepts, needs, and effective implementations of change management (the management of change and development within an organization) have never been in such high demand as they are now.

Why? We live in an era of major changes, transformations, and innovations – it is hard to keep up with everything that is directly affecting our life. Resisting changes with pushback and sabotage complicates problems even further.

But we see that all the time – everywhere we go. The sad part is, people are in more pain by self-sabotaging what at the end of the day will happen regardless. Early adapters are marching ahead, while others are left behind, risking to be obsolete in their way of thinking, acting, and performing in their working environments. Some of us do that masterfully in personal life and this reluctance, this hesitancy is bringing more conflicts, resentment, and pain.

> *"Failure is a resource. It helps you find the edge of your capacities."* ~ **Price Pritchett**

How is this applicable to you? If a girl like me could survive and then thrive in five different cultural, linguistic, educational, and geographical environments since she was almost 19 on her own, then you can too. I am no more special than you are. The only difference may be that I was daring and pushing myself every day a little further to do more while believing in myself that at the end of the day, everything would work out.

I learned without knowing at that time, how much I was relying on the unseen forces (unexpected and unknown resources yet to materialize) that Price so eloquently shared in his book you2: A High Velocity Formula for Multiplying Your Personal Effectiveness in Quantum Leaps. I don't want you guys to miss out on this powerful knowledge a day longer- You deserve to live a meaningful, powerful, and successful life regardless of your current situation, geographic location, or limited resources. Power is ultimately in your hands!

As it is a miracle for me to be alive and writing this book, it would be impossible for me to overcome "mission impossible" without relying on unseen forces so many times in my adult life.

"Just as real, though out of sight, an invisible resource ready to make a profound difference in what you can achieve."
~ Price Pritchett

The same applies to you – the fact that absence of evidence is not evidence of their absence, as Price shares so clearly in his book. How could this work for you too? As Price explains in his book and as I witnessed it to be true, these unseen forces seem to operate through our subconscious mind. It is a blend of our intuition, mental imagery, emotional engagement through visualization, and perhaps a sprinkle of "luck" or pure chance.

Somehow in some unexplained way, the resources, people, or support you need just seem to appear from nowhere or by coincidence. As you heard perhaps already from many thought-leaders, when you focus on things with a clear picture in our mind on what you want to accomplish, and you move in that direction positively and confidently, then you will allow the unseen forces to rally to your support. That is powerful, right?

My great friend Scott is a witness of some of the most amazing manifestations of this in my life, major breakthroughs, as well as the opportunities that shower me almost daily. He calls them "Bela's miracles" because he deeply believes that I am "attracting" them or co-creating them in my life. Either way, I am in deep gratitude every single day as a result of magic unfolding in front of my eyes that makes me believe more than ever before. The key is to be as specific with what you want to unfold in your life because, in the end, your beliefs will create your destiny.

Take Action:

Believing Within & In Unseen Forces

These questions are a means to better understand how to believe within yourself and discover unseen forces.

1. In times of struggle, what do you do? Do you look within yourself and others?

2. When others do not believe in you, do you struggle to believe in yourself?

Chapter Ten

Attaining Your Unwavering Faith

"Getting up and trying again and again is the secret of discovering what truly works on the path to success while mastering your Super Power!" ~ Izabela, **The World Messenger**

As I was packing to go to Puerto Vallarta, Mexico for a three week intensive immersion with locals in the city and backcountry, I could not shake off my excitement.

This trip was intended as an opportunity to immerse myself fully with the locals, and to mentally, physically, and emotionally prepare me for my bigger and longer trips to Sudan in East Africa and then Dharamsala in Northwest India. Both trips had a significant meaning in my life or at least this is what I thought in December of 2008.

During my time in Mexico, I spent hours practicing Spanish, walking on the beach, conversing as much as possible with local people. I saw such economic disparity between people who were living only several blocks away from each other. Walking alone by the beach before sunset one evening, I could not help but notice how happy local people were, smiling and joking with each other despite their hardships and how little they had. Kids played with each other on the beach while building sand castles and laughing.

Despite how careful I was to not get sick, the 7th day into my trip I experienced stomach symptoms to the point that I lost strength. I did not get better no matter what medicines I took from the local "pharmacy." Since I was not improving, I had to make a decision about the next possible steps and then take action. My options were to find strength before I got worse and packed up and return to the US. Or take a risk and stay in Mexico, not knowing if my condition would get worse. I decided that the first option to return to the US was the best thing for me to do immediately.

Regardless of how weak I was, I attempted to brighten myself with a bit of makeup and a small smile on my face and got a boarding pass for the late flight home that night.

Security was monitoring passengers closely and kept asking if any of us was feeling sick. I pretended that I was ok; I did not want security to prevent me from boarding that flight as it was my only hope to survive the stomach flu, and God knows what else I had.

I started visualizing that I was better despite my need to run to the bathroom every ten to fifteen minutes. I did not want to appear suspicious, so I sat on the floor, closed my eyes, and started meditating. I started feeling a little bit better and was running to the bathroom less frequently. When I finally boarded the airplane, I felt a huge sense of relief and slept like a baby as soon as we took off on the way to Denver.

When my uncle picked me up at the airport, he noticed that I looked snow white. During the trip, I had lost weight and was so weak that I could not even hold a conversation with him. I got home and took the longest hot shower of my life and slept for twenty-four hours straight. My body just wanted to rest, rest from my trip, but also in a way to prepare me for what was coming next. I was working intuitively to accept the magnitude of the upcoming change.

I had planned to go to Khartoum, Sudan to assist in opening the first non-profit hospital that I'd worked hard with others to make happen. Especially after participating alongside Mia Farrow and two male artists in the photographic exhibit, "Exhibit Darfur," during the Democratic National Convention in Denver.

I was drawn to do something else for the innocent children in Sudan. I was inspired after helping many local Denver based families from different parts of Sudan to rehabilitate and acculturate in a new environment after their escape from the horrors of genocide, war trauma, and torture.

"I was drawn to do more, something of significance for the innocent children in Sudan!" ~ Izabela, **The Word Messenger**

The Sudanese survivors I worked with represented another double-sided coin – political conflict resolution and the behind-the-scenes conflict infusion. At the time, I did not realize the depth of corruption and manipulation that was occurring in Sudan. It was not evident until later and looking back, if I had gone to Sudan at that time as planned, I most likely would have lost my life. The people whom I had trusted most were family members of one of the key ruling families in Sudan, many of whom had hidden agendas.

During this time, I received a painful call, informing me that my mom was taken to the emergency clinic in Zagreb with either a brain stroke or brain tumor. I sat on the floor of my bedroom and cried non-stop for hours in silence, solitude, and stillness. Tears rolled down my face like someone had opened the floodgates, blurring my vision, while my mind refused to accept this news.

Before I learned about my mom's terminal illness, I had planned out the whole upcoming year. I intended to spend three to four months in Sudan and then to continue my journey to Dharamsala, India. I had received exclusive clearance from Tibetan Headquarters in NYC to create a documentary with the Dali Lama, which was one of my biggest dreams. That dream existed ever since I spoke at the University of Denver in 2003, where His Holiness also spoke during the Peace Jam conference to youth from all over the world. Unfortunately, I had to put my dream on hold. At that time, I did not know for how long or if I would ever get another chance to make this documentary that I dreamed of.

At this time, my focus was on my mom. While I chose to not pursue my travels to Sudan and India, I was doing consulting work in the US and Europe. Working in Europe was an opportunity for me to spend as much time as I could with my mom, as I continued to hope that her Glioblastoma cancer would magically disappear. Unfortunately, it did not despite everyone's optimism, Reiki healing, endless prayers, visualizations, focused laser radiation therapy, and more than anything my mom's strong will to live.

My mom was an extraordinary woman to her last breath, always so optimistic. Celebrating my last birthday together with her, I brought her favorite Godiva Chocolate Cheesecake and Godiva Hazelnut coffee from the US. She passed away several days later, early on a Sunday morning. She had even arranged a special birthday cake for me from the local, cake shop while on her deathbed. To this day, I am deeply touched by her unconditional love that continued even into her final hours.

The night before she departed for the spiritual realm, I went to her favorite small Capuchin Franciscan church. I knelt in front of St. Mary's statue, feeling completely lost and defeated. But I prayed for my mom to die in peace and that God would put an end to her suffering as soon as possible.

"I never imagined in a million years that I would pray for someone I loved so much to die." ~ **Izabela, The World Messenger**

The next day, early in the morning as the sun rose, my mom took her final breath as small tears fell down her cheeks and her eyes fluttered open for a brief moment.

The rest of the year I spent in Europe, working, writing, and trying to cope with the loss of my mother. It took me awhile to realize that I was motherless and fatherless. I was, in fact, an orphan. I shed many tears of deep sorrow while I tried to regain my full inner strength. I found myself alone in an apartment in the central part of a small baroque city in Croatia, known as a city where angels sleep. How appropriate, I thought as I walked through small streets, wanting desperately to breathe in every moment that resembled or reminded me of the extraordinary woman I had called mom.

One day I found myself in front of the doors of a little church where my mom loved to go and stood in front of the big cross, looking at the Jesus statue.

I was drowning in the deepest sorrow and form of sadness, while I kept asking, "Now what? What do you want me to do?" But I was answered only with silence. Once again, I was broken and raw, wondering if I would ever be able to put myself back together.

During this time, my loving grandma Angela was my rock, my support as I was hers during the loss of her third child. How that felt for a mother, I can't even possibly imagine. I hope that I never have to find out in my lifetime.

I returned to the US around the holidays, before the end of 2010. I was getting ready to tackle the New Year with new clear goals and a renewed me. I spent the holidays with my only family in the US, my aunt and uncle and my two cousins, Romana and Rebecca. We were ready for magical 2011. I took many photos during the holidays, not knowing that they would be so significant months later.

Unfortunately, my world crashed again, just as I had picked myself back up from my mom's death. In January, a very good friend died from the same type of cancer as my mom, leaving behind a sweet four year old son and a heartbroken wife. I started to question again why this is happening and why God (or whoever is up there) is making these poor choices. Speaking at my friend's memorial was a hard thing for me to do emotionally. I had to speak in two languages, fully aware that the pain of his early departure opened up my wounds from the recent loss of my mom. But I could not say no to my friend when she asked me to speak. Honestly, I don't even know where the strength and clarity of mind came from when I delivered my speech at the memorial service.

Soon February started, and I experienced yet another heartbreak. The aunt I had shared holidays with started not feeling well and finally after a million appointments and tests; we learned that she had stage four pancreatic cancer. With this news, I could not pray, hope, or even believe that God or a version of a God existed. This time, it was just too much for me. Nothing made any sense.

As we were reviewing the options for the next steps for my aunt, I decided that I wanted to help in a different way, more practical and meaningful way. My aunt's liver was full of tumors, and it was failing. I wanted to buy her extra time with Rebecca, her 13 year old daughter. I had known before I started to do my physical tests that I would be the perfect donor. Sure enough I was. In my mind, I did not have anything to lose. I was single, without kids, and if something were to go wrong, I felt I would serve others well, too, since I was a registered organ donor. I was feeling a deep desire to improve my aunt's odds, regardless of the risks associated with the procedure.

I never got to be her donor. She lost a lot of weight while she was receiving her first chemo treatment. Her liver could not process any of the chemicals and released toxins into her body, fully wiping out her white blood cells. Her immune system was permanently destroyed. She continued to lose weight as her chemo treatment progressed. Soon it was as though I was looking at a ghost.

"The rapid human transformation that unfolded in front of my eyes was as if a fast-forwarded videotape was turning so quickly into the worst horror movie chilling me to the core."
~ Izabela, The World Messenger

She died in September of 2011, leaving a huge hole in so many lives. With her loss, and the previous losses I had endured, I felt like someone was playing a bad joke on me. Then, I looked at my sweet Rebecca, growing up and stepping up into adulthood too quickly, as I had done during the war. I made a promise to my aunt that I would stick around in Denver, Colorado until Rebecca at least graduated from high school regardless of what may happen in my life. I wanted her to know that she could have access to me 24/7 if she needed and that I am there for her, the only other relative on the continent besides her dad and older sister.

The following week after the funeral, I received a call from the doctor's office. I felt like a big wave had stricken me and that I was about to drown.

I collapsed for a moment until I found the strength to shake off the aftershock of the news. I was being asked to come to the office as the doctor needed to see me urgently.

I was beside myself. What was wrong with me? I had promised my aunt that I would look after Rebecca until she finished high school. I wondered how I would be able to do that now.

Sitting in the doctor's office, I realized that for the first time in my life something serious was going on with me. Really? I felt like I was living in a movie, and I had just been assigned this new role without even knowing what it was. I had to play along while more surprises were waiting for me on every corner.

I was informed that I had pre-cancerous and cancerous cells in my body, very early stage. What? Cancer in me? Impossible! I was convinced that they made a mistake – but they had not. How could it be? I eat healthy, I am positive, outgoing; my energy is consistently naturally high and positive, with an endless drive and zest for life. How could this be?

I asked for options and after listening to the various scenarios and recommendations, it was clear that I would not choose any aggressive treatment. My cancer had been caught early enough, so I elected to undergo a small procedure. It would heal quickly and would require frequent check-ups for three consecutive years, assuming I stayed cancer free!

Several days following my procedure, I went to my aunt's gravesite. It was there that my unwavering faith returned, and I knew that everything would be just fine. I now knew what I needed to do to get my life back on track. I gained more and more clarity. I knew I wasn't meant to die yet and that I had many plays left in me, big plays.

> *"Play bold, play bigger, and play full out!"*
> **~ Izabela, The World Messenger**

After the manifestation of the miracles in which I healed, continued to be cancer free. During this time, I also finished my master's degree, and worked on many fascinating projects. Unexpectedly, I lost the last rock in my life – my grandma, Angela.

My loving grandma died on Mother's Day in 2012. In the course of three years, I lost the most significant female members in my life and two friends. And I was saved, spared, and supported in the middle of all of it, standing alone to keep going, while providing emotional support to others within my family and to my closest friends.

I felt tested one more time in a way I never knew possible. I felt, even when I was uncertain why all of this was happening, that a power bigger and greater than me was showing me the way, and indirectly asking me to step up and step in, not to stop or hold back in any way.

I had a new and profound purpose that I needed to hold on to as the losses, healing, and uncomfortable situations were facing me on what seemed like a daily basis. And the purpose continued to evolve to include the desire to serve and support others even more than ever before. If I had not been willing to step in and step up as a liver donor for my terminally sick aunt to give her some extra time with her family, my cancer would not have been discovered. Even in negative situations, there is usually some positive aspect.

Instead of questioning why, I learned to surrender and go with the flow. I learned to be more patient and present while living a purposeful life. Through these experiences, I learned so much from others too, that ultimately led me to discover the secret of gratitude.

To me, gratitude is the never-ending process of self-discovery with a deep understanding of what we are capable of and how much we can be in touch within our surroundings and ourselves.

I remembered when I was asked the first time whether I saw the glass as half full or half empty. The first time a very negative person asked me that. I smiled and spontaneously said, "Of course half full.

Is it possible to be any other way?" The person looked at me with anger, not saying anything. I added politely, "In my world is not possible for it to be any other way." I refused to be pulled downward into an emotional spiral that would take so much effort to pull back up from.

There are moments when you have only two choices: either to magnify the negativity in your life or to dig deep to turn that misstep or issue into something positive and productive. You hold the key to success and achieving your goals. No one else has that power over you. One of the most profound quotes that keep echoing in my ears came from Henry Ford, who said, "He who believes he can and he who believes he cannot are both correct."

I remember when I was told that I am a dreamer and that I see the world through rose colored glasses. I laughed hard, practically shaking the windows in the small business office. I said being a dreamer not only helped me to survive but also to thrive and stand tall and proud like never before. The image of pink lenses never applied to me, but I had very sharp lenses with amazing zoom. I could in a second pick up photographic memories or snapshots. I had the capability to see things in front of me while registering so much data at any given moment. I learned how to be present, still, and aware. I learned how to be. To me, that is the most priceless skill or capacity that can take you so much further than any ride known to mankind.

Over time, I also developed a capacity to see more and share or say less. Just because I know something, I started to question whether I had to tell others. Is it useful, is it helpful, is it going to make a positive impact in their lives, are they ready to receive this information, is it my role to tell them? I realize that many people simply do not want to know. And ones who do – the ones who make it clear that they are ready and willing to listen – truly listen to hear and contemplate, not just to reply or defend.

The things that ultimately opened my world to the most profound way of being, in the deepest state of faith, were some of the most painful events to endure.

If I could use these events to change my life and to find greater purpose and meaning – then you can too if you choose to. When to start? My suggestion is

NOW! By doing only one thing differently right now, you can start unfolding a whole new life.

As you can imagine, I often questioned my ability to have faith again, especially after all of the losses I endured. But after I started to hope again, and then believed in myself again, faith came as an wise old man knocking on my door of shame, solitude, sadness, and stillness. During this lonely time I could not for the life of me pray. I would look blank, would not even know what to be grateful for until I started practicing my prayer in a new more purposeful way. I prayed when everything started to be good again. I did not pray from desperation or fear as I had many times before. Now I prayed from a place of gratitude and profound joy for what I had. By giving thanks for what I got, things shifted quickly for me.

As soon as you start experiencing self-doubt or fear, you can take control, you can intervene and change your thoughts, by transforming them from fear to faith. When you are in this state, you are allowing magic to happen. The state of faith is the beginning of all great achievements. So why not let yourself and your mission unfold as fast as possible?

"The state of faith is the beginning of all great achievements!"
~ Izabela, The World Messenger

Take Action:

Attaining Your Unwavering Faith

Use these questions to help you identify what you believe in so that you can develop and unwavering faith for it. Note: This doesn't have to be religious based faith, rather is an unshakable truth that you hold true.

1. What do you believe in?

2. What distractions can you eliminate from your path to faith, to fully comprehend what you believe in?

Chapter Eleven

Pursuing Your Destiny & Leaving Your Legacy

As I am finishing the final pages of the book, I can't help but smile as I reflect on my life journey thus far. Looking at today and ahead, my future is very bright. I am already working on my next book and elite professional athlete and executive training programs. The best part, there is already demand for it not only in the US but also in Europe, the Middle East, and other parts of the world.

The concept of legacy leadership, leading in our unique legendary way, is very powerful because it gives us a mindful focus to our mission, our values, and our desire for long-term impact. At the same time, it influences how we approach what we do every single day.

The key is to be authentic and consistent, true to yourself, and to adjust or adopt accordingly. As many of our past events shaped us into who we are today, today's events will shape us into who we will become tomorrow. The best part is that we can use our internal power and self-awareness in helping ourselves reach our full potential and much more. Destiny is a choice as well as a legacy. Together, they are so interconnected, intertwined like the moon and stars, if you aim to reach a star, then you can reach the moon too. If you are the dreamer like me, why would you satisfy your thirst with something so limiting when you can have a whole galaxy?

On your path to reach your dreams while you uncover living your life to the fullest, you will discover your destiny. The best part is that we are the masters of our own destiny. We are the ones who hold the keys to our true potential where we can decide how we want to play in life. It is not the length or the quantity, but the excellence and the quality that matter in life.

Recently, I was asked by a passionate young man eager to get his life in order if destiny is similar to goal setting. It is a stepping-stone or a practice of creating your true, purposeful life. Living life without clear goals is like living a life without a deep meaning. Think about how you can expand from small goals and a wide range of goals to big life goals, with a true mission and purpose. Plan to fulfill our dreams.

That will get you excited and on the right track with a game plan to succeed in life. When you live your life with purpose and mission, it gives your life special meaning. That meaning extends further and deeper over time, and guess what happens next? You will be blasting through knowing exactly where you are going and what you are doing. The best part is that you will no longer feel lost or feel like you are wasting your time.

How do we truly pursue our destiny? In short, by developing our "life attitude" that will allow us to do more than conquering major obstacles in our life and then by reaching our biggest goals. It is an attitude that allows us to finish our life course while truly enjoying the journey of choice and attaining the beauty of our dreams and deepest desires. As we continue to grow and further develop in all aspects of our lives, especially after reaching a higher level of emotional intelligence, life with unlimited possibilities will start to unfold. You will be so well equipped to make great decisions that you will be propelled further on your path to your destiny than you ever imagined possible. One of the main reasons that I am sharing some very painful and challenging experiences with you is to show you how I arrived at where I am today: aware of a purpose and mission that suggested direction. It does not mean that pain and suffering are the best teachers of them all – although they can handle in constructive and helpful ways.

You, too, can get there as fast as you want depending on how truly important it is to you. More than ever we need to be authentic and vulnerable, as well as genuine, and upfront with others and ourselves. Today, people speak only one quarter of the truth up front. Only one half when they are trying to get what they want, while they share the whole truth when in deep trouble (or a close version of it to justify their actions). The sad part is that more adults in their forties are acting this way, especially in business. I always wonder how this is possible. What happened to their upbringing and morals? Where is their leadership compass? Why are they so stingy with the truth?

During my liberating, freeing, and exciting journey, I developed ten new habits that have helped me stay focused and have also enabled me to reach my path to destiny faster. You are invited to following these Ten Steps to Reach Your Destiny:

1: Unearth a new depth and capacity to love. To love no matter what, unconditionally, freely. That sweet feeling in your body, mind, heart, spirit, and whole being that makes your world go around faster until you find yourself spinning and breathless.

2: Unleash your capacity to feel joy. As a result, you will find yourself skipping. Yes, skipping as I used to as a six year old. It puts a sweet smile on my face and warmth in my heart. (When I skip – and I still do – I honestly don't care who is watching or what they may think.)

3: Wake up every morning with deep gratitude for one more day to make a positive impact in this world. Doing something of significance is so rewarding and endlessly satisfying that it gets me to jump out of bed early, often before Jack, my dog, comes to give me a wake-up lick on my cheek.

4: Expect daily miracles to occur in your life. Small, big, huge – any or all, just expect miracles in each day. Why? You deserve them. You are good enough. You earned them. Believe in miracles.

5: Meditate or reflect every morning. Find a quiet place so you can arm yourself with your Super Power and prepare yourself to conquer the day.

6: Seek at least one full-hearted laugh out loud (LOL) moment each day. I even post them on Facebook with the aim to remind my friends to laugh; laughing after all is important on the path to greatness. Simply sharing humor is a simple way to reach many people in a positive, loving way, whether they are down or already having a great day.

7: Create healthy meals to nourish your body. I cook and constantly seek nutritious meals for my body. Breakfast is particularly important as it is the foundation for creating energy that just keeps circulating as I progress with my day.

8: Exercise every day, even if only for 20-30 minutes. Walk and talk with your peers, mentors, and friends – it saves you time and allows you to create deeper bonds and connections.

9: Commit to learning something new every single day. The best way to do so is by asking questions or communicating with one of your mentors, teammates, or friends, or even a complete stranger – or through reading. I read and learn a lot on a wide range of topics on my own, but the best learning experiences I have had so far are directly from other human beings.

10: Write unique and original content on topics that you are an expert on or simply so passionate about that you just can't wait to share it with the world. Be bold and be visible! Engage with others and make a difference. Make yourself approachable, reachable, and caring. Shine on, sunshine!

"When you are fully utilizing your passion in sports, business, or life, you will be ready to be fully motivated, dedicated, and committed!" ~ Izabela, The World Messenger

Way too many people succumb to the fear and highly irrational idea that their destiny is predetermined, so they simply give up or surrender themselves to whatever it may be. This leads to people believing that they are destined to fail or succeed.

Please hear me loud and clear: Make no mistake about it. Your destiny is in your own hands! If you are blaming multiple successes or failures on forces that are "beyond your control" it is nothing more than a cop out. You are better and greater than that. You can always make a better decision next time around.

Decisions that we make navigate and select the direction of our life ultimately determine our destiny. It is simple as that.

"Decisions that we make navigate and select the direction of our life and ultimately determine our destiny!
~ Izabela, The World Messenger

As you have heard from my personal story, sometimes life will deal you difficult cards to play, with very few options, and at other times you will be holding aces and some extra jokers too. Your personal willingness to give it your best and to give it your all in playing any hand will determine your ultimate success or failure in life.

Through these experiences, I was able to realize that there is more to life than we thought early on in life, even during college. The key is to allow yourself to experience life.

As I reflect on my work with the extraordinary people I have encountered from around the world, including refugees, war trauma, torture, and genocide survivors, I recognized connections that transcend culture, language, race, age, gender, status, profession, or education. There was a profound blend of acceptance, compassion, kindness, generosity, and openness.

I also learned something profound through this process that is essential to generate in your life: Independence.

The force to stand on our own two feet without any, or very little, support from anyone else at the most transformational parts of our life can give us the strength to carry on during the times of our biggest challenges and defeats.

Many of us virtually had no, or a very short, childhood. Adult life came too quickly with all of its responsibilities where many of us forgot to remember to be playful, joyful or to enjoy simple pleasures that life offers so generously.

The power of discovering that sweet inner child in everyone of us, helps us remember what our true dreams are to pursue our destiny.

Further, so many of us were reprogrammed to not listen to our gut even in our adulthood. As children, we experienced many things that were going wrong, but adults told us that everything was all right. So naturally, we detach from our gut feeling or we learn how to ignore it or simply to doubt what our gut feeling is telling us. Does this sound familiar? We can change this at any time.

By accepting who we are versus who we should be, we increase the probability of our success by investing our energy and effort in what matters most: our real selves.

When we feel with our hearts, we open ourselves to feel the most powerful force, energy, an essence of who we are as a whole, unlocking the pathway to the soul. The soul's drive is the deepest part of a person's personality, and it is the most important. Why? It unlocks the Super Power hidden within each one of us. It unlocks the most amazing source of energy.

Unfortunately, many people are not in touch with that energy. In fact, some people never get in touch with their soul's energy. I am sure you see as I did so many people "walking dead" in their corporate jobs. Jobs that they hate, or enslaved in toxic environments, confined to negative actions, such as war, terror, aggression, or abuse.

What they are missing are the true, natural life juices that will keep them alive beyond basic body nourishment. What people often forget is that soul energy creates a drive – a deep yearning and inner knowledge. Of all the different energy parts of our personality, the soul energy is the most important to fulfill to achieve true greatness in life. This energy keeps us internally youthful, passionate about life, positive, and enthusiastic.

When you fully harness this amazing energy, you are open and fully onboard to reach not only your full potential but to accomplish your destiny.

Based on my numerous conversations with spiritual leaders from all walks of life, through magnificent exposure to people from around the globe, I found one more undeniable thread not only in our beliefs but also in our actions.

Everyone is born with the ability to choose their destiny and develop a purpose. Sure, there may be fear or hesitation about doing what you came here to do, and that is perfectly fine. When you are fully ready – you will simply know, and it will feel magical.

Often our destiny may not be something we want to fulfill but something we need to learn to do anything else in life. But the key to doing this is not something you seek outside of yourself. It is something you seek within – it is your emotional capacity that will hold you either a hostage or will set you free to soar like an eagle. Beautiful people with equally beautiful minds and hearts offered their unconditional love and support as my journey as The World Messenger began with the formation and creation of this book. It echoes with what our society needs the most today. A deep awareness of self, love, truth, and God (or whoever that may be in your world, the source bigger and greater than you).

If you get one step closer in the self-discovery process regardless if you are thirteen and you have not yet done much or if you are forty three lost on your path to greatness, confused, or starting over, consider that step tremendous progress.

By coming closer to finding the answer it can take you on the most extraordinary ride of your life if you are truly ready.
Leave your fear behind.

Know that every word in this book was given to you with unconditional love and hope for understanding each other.

"When we walk alone, we find profound solitude, but when we walk together we find LOVE!" ~ Izabela, The World Messenger

The supreme path to your destiny lies in the active role of leadership by serving others. This can be accomplished by designing a life of substance, purpose, and meaning. And this can't be done alone!

This effort can set you up to live the most profound life, by creating a legacy, however, small or big you choose it to be.

Take Action:

Pursuing Your Destiny & Leaving Your Legacy

I encourage you to find out how you can pursue your destiny and leave a legacy by answering these questions below.

1. How do you want to impact those around you and those to come when you are no longer here?

2. What specific steps do you need to take to achieve impact while you are living and for when you are gone?

Chapter Twelve

Inspiring Greatness By Leading Your Legendary Way

"Greatness is achieved at the moment we start making a positive difference in other people's lives by providing the most valuable service with the highest impact."
~ Izabela, The World Messenger

As a teen who loved to listen to MTV, via small satellite antenna, I was so inspired by British pop culture and good old classics from The Beatles era. Some teens around me grew up on folk music while others like me grew up on U2, Prince, Michael Jackson, Annie Lenox, and many more. I loved music, fashion, travel, magazines, and sports. Later, I started liking boys too. Somehow, no one shared with me how it should feel until it was too late. My big brave heart that I wore on my sleeve during my teenage years was somehow always wounded; sometimes just a little bit and other times with very deep painful cuts.

"To live up to your greatness you must master your emotional intelligence." **~ Izabela, The World Messenger**

At that time, I did not know how to "evaluate" boys and each respective situation to see who was real and who was a "player." As my life progressed, I faced other intense events. I soon found myself on a mission to further develop my emotional intelligence (EI).

"Emotional Intelligence" was originally developed by Peter Salovey, Ph. D. (now President of Yale University) with John D. Mayer. Here is a link to their original work before it was popularized in bestselling books: http://goo.gl/Hqu4Pf.

I believed early on that EI could carry me through anything. Through the life experiences that I had, that proved to be true. Years later, thanks to mastering EI, I can quickly assess the situation of my surroundings for any event and adjust my behavior accordingly. I discovered EI was an essential ingredient on my path towards greatness. EI is an extremely powerful tool that can be utilized not only personally, as well as professionally.

On the personal side, nothing is more energizing than two people constantly growing and pushing each other to be the best they can be. If you have already found that special "partner in crime" that we all seek to support us during the many unexpected rollercoaster rides of life, you should consider yourself the luckiest person in the world and make sure you nurture that relationship every single day. Feel the gratitude for all that you have and have created together as a result of it! I was fortunate to have had that in my life at one point, and I know how valuable and precious such a relationship is.

However if you are in the group that is not there yet but seeking or searching for that very special someone (possibly, again), then you may want to consider believing the following: It will happen, you just have to be open and go with the flow. Do not "settle" just because it is not happening the way you want, how you want it, and when you want it. Some things just can't be rushed or ordered on Amazon and shipped to your home to satisfy your need for instant gratification like getting a new pair of shoes or a car gadget.

As I interact with youth, I often get asked not only about the lessons I've learned, but also about any regrets that I may have thus far in my life. Regrets? Oh, yes. I wished that I played more with my friends, got more scars (trophies) while playing soccer with them, spent more time with the people in my life who truly mattered, and told those people more often how much I loved them.

I wish I had danced more after I stopped playing sports and enrolled in dance school. I mastered modern dancing as my regular workout routine during my dance marathons as a teenager. The word diet was not in my vocabulary until I moved to the US.

I wish I had been more bold and daring to explore bigger opportunities whenever I was told, "you are too young, Bela." Often I wondered, "But what if it will be too late?" My life would be so different if I were allowed to go to England right after high school.

I had an opportunity to work and go to school there, but that was quickly shot down by some of my family members advising my mom against it. Why? The door was locked too quickly before I could even explore the open door. I was so disappointed that at that time I just simply couldn't wait to take my life into my hands. After all, my dad was the sheriff in the house, even though he was often disguised under the strong leadership and influence of my mom.

I also wished I listened to my gut whenever I was making an important decision even when my perspective was different from the people who I knew I could trust unconditionally. Don't take me wrong – my life was great and very rich in so many ways for which I am grateful.

Through many painful lessons in life, I learned this profound truth: meet people where they are at, instead of where they could be or are falling short of reaching their potential. So many people have endless opportunities to grow and get better, yet they don't act on them. This is truly a profound lesson on the path to greatness.

We have only one life to live regardless of what we are going through at the moment. The key is to make the best of it. Each one of us has a unique gift to give and share with others. But you have to be ready to share, learn, and grow. Otherwise, it is just potential. To uncork the untapped potential, we must desire, want, and act on the inner potential so we can each be the best we can be.

"Meet people where they are instead of where they could be when making important decisions; then inspire them to reach their true potential!" ~ Izabela, The World Messenger

When we step forward in our truth and embrace life fully, then truly amazing things start to unfold. As we step into more and more greatness within us despite our current situations, challenges or obstacles, then we start attracting more greatness around us. People and possibilities for a meaningful life start unfolding fast in all aspects of our lives.

On a professional level, through my numerous conversations and experiences in business, I learned that rooms are often filled with highly intelligent people. Most of them came from prestigious universities, with MBA degrees and a handful of new and trendy certifications and courses. But that doesn't guarantee that they are emotionally intelligent. By sitting and observing the room of people, I could quickly identify their EI or better yet lack of it, based on their body language, word usage, and overall team dynamics. As a result, I can predict the outcomes of choices and decisions that they will make.

In the business world, the connection between EI and high performance is finally being recognized. Today, more and more companies are accepting the importance of EI, and have incorporated a wide range of EI tests into a part of the interview and talent prescreening process as well as once hired as part of professional development. It is not surprising to see how the connection between earning potential and overall higher marks on annual performance evaluations are significantly higher for peers with more developed EI. What a great motivator, right? To establish high performing teams, it is crucial for leadership to demonstrate and integrate high EI in the working environment.

As I spoke with a wide range of professional athletes, it was hard not to see a common thread between them and business leaders. The performance was the key factor of an individual athlete's success and their contribution to the team. Their emotional awareness, including their ability to identify their own, and in other players, leads them to make the most important decisions, adjust their performance, and play their best.

"In sport the highs are very high and the lows are very low but always put the sport at the heart of everything you do."
~ Roger Draper

They could not emphasize strongly enough the importance to always play your hardest, regardless of the situation you may be in, by consistently delivering high performance and exceptional individual contributions. At the end of the day, you will not have any reason to lose a good night of sleep, or to question and wonder "what if," nor to self-judge, self-abuse, or live with regrets. But to do that, we need to work on self-mastery.

"Greatness is accomplished when we truly grasp our inner world." ~ Izabela, The World Messenger

Establish deep connections within yourself, your inner world – your body, mind, spirit, and emotions, so that you can create your path to greatness. You must be willing to invest in yourself before someone else will.

You must be your own champion before you win championships.

"To achieve high performance impact you must engage your body, mind, spirit, and emotions." ~ Izabela, The World Messenger

During the uncertain pre-Balkan war times, I felt more than ever the embodiment of John Lennon's famous saying, "Life is what happens to you while you are busy making plans." I caught myself making plans; I could not help it. For example, I would calculate how quickly I could get through college, what my next travel destination would be, what school I would teach at, what my next trip would be, and what I would buy with my first paycheck. I had a million goals, ideas, dreams, and inspirations. At that time I was fearless and ready to do almost anything, just like Roger Bannister, the British runner who ran the first four-minute mile. Before that moment in 1954, no one thought that this was possible. His record lasted only 46 days and after Roger proved it could be done, everyone else followed suit, because they believed they could match or better his achievement.

I also wanted to break some old records or limited beliefs, and quickly create new ones in different disciplines that are equally or even more important through the power of high performance impact.

"To know what is possible, we need to seek, embrace, and act on the impossible." ~ Izabela, **The World Messenger**

So to better understand the impact of lacking internal potential, I spent some time with Leon Smith, the British Men's Tennis Captain. He has trained elite players since 1998. Leon originally started as a playing companion to Andy Murray. Gradually, Leon transitioned into more of a coaching role while Andy progressed with his tennis career. Leon was very intuitive, and he was able to contribute significantly to the early development of multiple professional players in the UK by trusting his instincts.

The story behind Leon's success is attributed to his willingness and openness to take on tennis in a role as a coach rather than as a player. Over time, he was able to form and frame his coaching strategy and style. His high level of commitment to the players he coached was essential to his success.

"It is so important to know what stage the players are in their professional career to know what type of coaching they need the most to succeed." ~ **Leon Smith**

In general, the UK coaching program is not as highly regulated as it is in France or other countries. That helped Leon to excel quickly after an early self-realization that he was not going to be a successful professional tennis player. Due to his high EI, he was able to shift immediately his attention to becoming a professional tennis coach and seize new opportunities. In different stages of professional development especially, we depend so much on mentors and coaches to identify growth opportunities as well as what is hindering our growth on the path to greatness.

As Leon knows well, if too many things change simultaneously too often, then it is hard to know what is working well and why. It is essential to know what changes are necessary at different stages of a player's professional life. Not all players are alike, and change requires careful consideration of each player and individualized implementation for success.

"Be good at what you do and focus on the outcomes and achievements of your work and how this is communicated to sporting people." ~ Roger Draper

When Roger Draper, the former CEO of Law Tennis Association (LTA), nominated and selected Leon Smith, a young coach, over the more seasoned coaches and retired professional players for the LTA's Head of Men's Tennis as well as captain of the Great Britain Davis Cup team, there was a lot of initial pushback. News coverage slammed Roger and Leon. Despite the negative press coverage that ensued for the first six to twelve months, Roger stood his ground. Press and attention in UK tennis coverage are more intense than in the US; in fact, it is similar to NFL coverage and exposure. Roger's leadership was questioned during "unpopular" times, but his decision to promote Leon ultimately proved to be one that benefitted the players and British tennis in general and soon the press had to change its tune.

Roger himself has a very interesting life story that got him on the path to greatness early on. He is a veteran in a wide range of sports, including professional rugby and tennis at a high level. He was always very frustrated at how badly sports, in general, were managed in the UK. He was on a mission to improve and further develop sports management after he finished his professional career. Roger is an exceptional human being that I am very proud to know, in addition to a being fantastic mentor, coach, father, husband, and friend. His son Jack is a very promising future UK tennis star. I am eager to watch his progress in the years to come.

Don't spend too much time responding to cynical people who are not aligned to what you want to achieve. **~ Roger Draper**

One of the great lessons that Roger shared with me was never to settle for the status quo. In addition, he learned firsthand that if you want to transform sport, expect to experience at times frustration, friendship, anger, disbelief, enjoyment, a sense of being let down and a lack of praise and recognition.

"In sport the highs are very high and the lows are very low but always put the sport at the heart of everything you do." **~ Roger Draper**

Roger served for 13 years as chief executive for such major projects as the Olympic bid and Wimbledon stadium. His experiences afforded him the opportunity to gather insights across all Olympic sports from world-class professional athletes and coaches. As a result of his efforts and his vision to reach greatness, he turned professional sports management around in the UK. Obviously they haven't won Wimbledon, but they won the rugby world cup and the cricket world cup, and the Olympics were a huge success, as were the Para-Olympics.

"Spend most of your time listening to and working with people that share you passion." **~ Roger Draper**

Life is too short to deny yourself the opportunity to be the best you can be. For athletes to succeed, they need to be adaptive, and they need to learn their sport. But they also need to have support and engagement with their coaches and teammates as Flo Pietzsch, Strength and Conditioning Coach and Senior Lecturer in Sports Coaching at the University of Brighton shared with me.

Flo has worked across many sports including rugby, cricket, and professional tennis. In addition, he provided support to the Great Britain Fed Cup team and as result he has extremely powerful insight into these sports.

There are a lot of different coaching styles and not all of them work for everyone. The key is to try things out, see what works and what does not, adjust as needed, and then keep going. As every sport is unique they require different approaches. Some are more technical and rarely adopt science, while others do not.

The best evidence of that is a British cycling success story that employed several top scientists who looked at critically evaluating the performance of athletes from a scientific standpoint. Sadly, other sports are not yet even taking this into consideration and are still coaching and training old school.

Flo has often witnessed what it is possible to accomplish with individuals and teams with high EI and a desire for greatness. The successful teams usually share these characteristics:

- Individual and team motivation and contribution
- Shared focus
- Shared goals
- Excellent team communication
- Leadership
- A wide range of skilled, innovative coaches

It is exciting how far players and coaches will be reaching with new and innovative training programs.

I can't wait to see impact created by the High Performance Impact Evolution ™ in sports, business and life! Game on Champions!!!

Take Action:

Inspiring Greatness by Leading Your Legendary Way

Please use these questions to understand how you can inspire greatness and lead in a legendary way.

1. What does greatness means to you?

2. How can you inspire those around you by doing what you love and are great most?

Chapter Thirteen

Applying
The World Messenger's Legacy

By now you may be very clear that everything in our lives personally and professionally falls and rises on leadership. As you discover more about yourself and how you are leading or wish to lead, think about the legacy you would like to leave behind. Think not only when you are gone from the planet earth, but while you are still living and aiming to accomplish greater things in your life.

You may be wondering how to know if you are headed in the right direction or if you are having an impact, or even if you are offering true value to others. Trust me, you are not alone in pondering these questions.

Your Leadership Legacy is all about learning from your past experiences, living life to the fullest at the moment, and building for the future. Leadership Legacy is also about finding deeper meaning in life while positively impacting others.

> *"Live your life with purpose by leaving a legacy to a brighter future."* ~ **Izabela, The World Messenger**

Leadership Legacy is not bound by age or socio-economic status. It represents a body of work at each stage of your journey. Your Leadership Legacy expands with each new experience, or new bold idea, or innovation that you courageously acted on that inspired others to do the same. There is nothing more important, rewarding or fulfilling than to contribute in such a meaningful and positive way.

People often don't make meaningful contributions because it is hard for them to measure the impact of their actions. Others focus on the end of their career or life as the time to leave that legacy. The truth is that Legacy Leadership is an integral part of your day-to-day work at any stage of your life and career, wherever and whenever you contributed value, growth, innovation and an opportunity to others.

How powerful this is, right? Just because you are not winning the moment you start to play, it does not mean that you can't ultimately win the game!

Many have asked me how to create Legacy Leadership that starts now, and that will last beyond their career or lifetime. Legacy occurs when you create a climate of leadership through your organization and in your personal life. Simply put, the magic of Legacy Leadership can be calculated by this simple yet profound formula, thanks to the leadership of Dennis Pitocco:

Legacy Leadership = Impact x Breadth x Duration x Multiplicity

Impact – how much you improve things. We all need improvement on personal and professional levels. The key is to know what and how to reach high performance impact.

Breadth – measures how far your reach extends. With today's technologies accessible to almost anyone, you can achieve a global impact rather fast. The key is to offer a valuable solution, invention, information, or service. With that, you will be amazed how your scope and scale of reach may expand.

Duration – calculates how far what you build today will carry into the future. Indeed, a select number of leaders see their legacies unfold during their lifetimes, to last long after they are gone. Whether it is a company or a country (think Steve Jobs and Nelson Mandela), their work and vision endures.

Multiplicity – is all about how much those who follow you build upon the things you have created. Can anyone duplicate your results, and do even better? This is not the hype or quick win. Instead, it is leading with a consistent value over a long time, in fact, over your lifetime.

For those of you who are hungry for more information on Legacy Leadership, eager and ready to start building your enduring legacy, please feel free to subscribe to my Legacy Leadership EXECUBRIEFS (http://bizcatalyst360.com/free-execubriefs/). This is an excellent forum to ask questions, provide feedback, and share with others your magical experience on the path to Legacy Leadership.

"The most profound life and leadership lessons are threaded with hundreds of colorful tapestries of cultures that echo their words of wisdom." ~ Izabela, The World Messenger

A remarkable example I have found is how similarly three very different cultures, religions, and geographic regions define a person's success at the true art of leadership! As I listened to the voices of a Native American Chief, a Sufi Master, and a Buddhist Monk share their respective stories, I couldn't help but smile and feel a universal truth about measuring our leadership success. It all boiled down to three themes:

Raise a child or children – Or simply help others to raise them well. You can start doing your part today. What a great opportunity to not only help children (whether they are yours or not) to grow, but also to coach them early on to be competent, confident, and capable. Words and actions of support and encouragement will mean a lot to them as they are growing and gaining more life experience. By praising their effort, modeling positive self-talk (internal dialog), teaching them self-encouragement, and loving them unconditionally, you can give a child the leadership skills that YOU use every day in business. Big kudos to all teachers, coaches, and mentors who are willing to invest that extra mile when no one else is.

Plant a tree or trees – Invest in your neighborhood, community and forge a green legacy for future generations to enjoy today. In addition to the beauty, health, and quality of life that trees offer, we can't forget the environmental implications that we are facing today and in years to come.

Daydreaming and playing chess underneath over a 100 year-old tree is an absolutely priceless experience. Do you sometimes wonder what trees, parks, or mountains the voices of your children and grandchildren will one day echo? The fact is that we are enjoying today magnificent shade in the hot summers because someone planted trees a long time ago.

"Let's pay it forward to generations yet to come by planting trees as a part of our legacy!" ~ Izabela, The World Messenger

Write a book or books – Pass on your wisdom today. You may not simply get another chance. When you are passionate about a topic (as I am about legacy leadership) find ways to share your expertise with others through a blog post or email. I've always wondered why more successful athletes and business leaders who I've met do not write their own blog or book. It is an excellent avenue to establish yourself as an authority on a topic, expand your market, and add tremendous value to others beyond your title, company name, or award.

In 2005, as I was standing downtown Toronto before Central Station, a river of people poured out, moving so fast in so many directions, like little ants, showering me with the most amazing energy. The sounds of different voices, accents, languages, and the mix of faces representing virtually every nation was like taking a trip around the world.

"As I am standing still in the epicenter of the world, its profound beauty showered me to the core with the most delightful energy." ~ Izabela, The World Messenger

This experience in Toronto, after traveling to over 40 countries, and visiting numerous large cities, including New York, was the most profound connection I felt thus far. Why? I was one hundred percent present, standing in the silence, simply observing.

I saw hundreds of different ethnic groups, languages, people dressed in their own unique cultural outfits, walking and interacting in ways culturally appropriate to their standards. Some smiled, some gestured as they talked, some walked fast with serious thoughts on their mind, some held each other's hands expressing love and affection, and some simply slowed down as they had just finished their work, deciding where to go next before heading home.

The words of my childhood hero, the great Muhammad Ali, "To succeed we need the skill and the will, but the will should always be higher than the skill" echo to this day in my head. Indeed, where there is a will, then there is a way to accomplish anything you desire in your life.

"Mastering the art of leadership through business, sports or life is the essence of lasting success that naturally leads you to the creation of a timeless legacy." ~ **Izabela, The World Messenger**

Truth be told, mastering the art of leadership can't be done without constant learning. Constant learning is a daily practice; it requires continuous personal effort. Allowing ourselves to hear things we are not always happy about, but to hear them anyway, is a sign of deep progress. Through this process, we can learn how to be fearless by facing current realities or problems with a new attitude and the ability to take decisive action, all while fully committing and taking full responsibility for the outcome.

But to reach our goal faster, we must anticipate our success. As many of you were anticipating my book, I started to anticipate its impact on your personal and professional life. That is why I spent months interviewing powerful sports figures and coaches in addition to some of the most innovative minds in the business. My wish for you is that you consider their ideas and lives and remind yourself, or decide for yourself, what you are doing right now.

We often shy away from what people tell us that we don't want to hear but need to hear the most, who point out things that they see that we don't want to see. It is difficult to hear from people who tell us who we can be, especially when they are reminding us of a dream that we abandoned.

When you find yourself in moments surrounded by darkness, hold onto your Olympic torch.

Let that light show you the possibilities and endless paths that you can take. My wish for you is that you select the possibilities and paths that get you closer to your dream!

You will need a personal will and effort combined with a positive attitude. Even if your path is not clear or apparent to you at the moment, you are pursuing your life of meaning while leaving your destiny. Things will fall in place more and more as you become clearer on what you seek in and from life.

"Your passion and love for the game and deep desire for success must be greater than the sum of self-doubt, criticism, uncertainty, and failure combined."
~ Izabela, The World Messenger

My purpose in writing this book was to convey the experiences and lessons that I have learned through my journey and the lessons learned by many athletes and executives I interviewed. Hopefully it is offering you some comfort, perspective, and guidance to assist you, whether you are lost, lonely, defeated, or just looking to further your personal and professional journey.

As I close a chapter in my life with the writing of this book, I am opening up a new one. I will be working side by side with some of the most inspiring & influential people who create positive change in and around our world.

My goal is to leave a lasting legacy in the form of personal and online interactions with people from around the globe. To do this in a big and meaningful way, I will be offering leadership life-changing seminars, consulting, and training, as well as volunteer work to help those in need. Join me in creating over one million legacy leaders around the world!

My goal with you is to help you to feel supported during moments of hardship or struggle. I want you to understand that you can indeed overcome anything and have anything you want in life.

Your dreams can come true! Through our sincere and honest sharing in today's online world, you can connect with others in a more personal, meaningful, and profound way while having a huge impact on the lives of others. I humbly want to connect with you, as well as you with me, through my writing, with the aim of improving the wellbeing of others. Feel free to reach out directly to me on LinkedIn and my website IzabelaLundberg.com. Also, through Amazon, by leaving your comments about the book, its impact, and what you found to be most useful from The World Messenger.

My dream is to create over one million legacy leaders in my lifetime. The best way to start that dream is to partner with like-minded visionary leaders that have a deep desire to make a positive impact and share the similar vision. If you are one of them, feel free to reach directly to me at IzabelaLundberg.com under Contact and Partnership Opportunities.

My hope is that by the time you have finished reading this book, you will possess more than ever the will, the passion, and the Super Powers to achieve your path to greatness.

"Be proud of the place that you live in, as well as being the pride of where you live!" ~ Izabela, **The World Messenger**

Take Action:

Applying The World Messenger's Legacy

Use these questions to discover how you can apply what you've learned in my book to your daily life.

1. Which of my personal stories resonated with you most and why? What did you learn from it and how do you plan to apply this in your life?

2. Which of my interviews of sports and business professionals inspired you? How will the information from the interview(s) help you achieve your goals?

MIRACLES

As the sun rises on the horizon, it is announcing a new day with a renewed zest for life. The World Messenger took a deep breath while enjoying the warmth of the sun on her skin, smiling.

With deep reflection and gratitude to her ancestry, deeply rooted and dated to Queen Katarina, known as the "people's queen." Her message is yet to unfold the legacy of many ancestors who gave their lives and paid a high price for their short-lived freedom century after century.

There is a history of strong woman warriors, generation after generation, who lived in exile while seeking freedom. A freedom fought for with undying love, deep compassion, and wisdom, continually spreading the seeds of love in every act and decision made through the centuries. The old prophecy will unfold only through Global Citizenship and when harmony transcends the world, The World Messenger will return.

The End

ABOUT THE AUTHOR

 Izabela Lundberg is an internationally recognized consultant, facilitator, speaker, writer, humanitarian, and immigrant entrepreneur whose clients include subject matter experts and Fortune 500 companies. She is well known for her writing on High Performance Impact in business and sports and is a leading authority on High Performance Impact Leadership. Ms. Lundberg generates tremendous value and delivers exceptional results for her global clients and audience.

Ms. Lundberg enjoys a dynamic worldview after living in six countries, speaking six languages, traveling to over 40 countries, and working with diverse teams from over 80 countries. She is a recognized catalyst of sustainable solutions for global leaders and their most pressing challenges.

As survivor of some of the worst human atrocities – genocide, torture and war trauma – she has also championed other survivors around the world to restore their dreams, find their voice, and tap into their highest potential through art, holistic healing, and leadership training.

You can find Ms. Lundberg at:
www.IzabelaLundberg.com and
http://www.linkedin.com/in/izabelalundberg.

CONTACT THE AUTHOR

Now that you have read The World Messenger, do you want to learn more? Do you want assistance assessing, guiding, and inspiring your teams? In addition to the content of this book, Ms. Lundberg has developed self-assessment evaluations, guides, and other tools for purchase.

The content can be tailored to meet your needs. Ms. Lundberg has worked with many types of people and groups, from businesses to athletic organizations and from war survivors to youth. She is also available to conduct in-person or virtual sessions for individuals, small groups, and organizations.

Please contact Ms. Lundberg at www.izabelalundberg.com. She looks forward to receiving your inquiries and helping you achieve your goals.

Made in the USA
San Bernardino, CA
03 June 2019